On Being Mad or Merely Angry

_____

Books by James W. Clarke

American Assassins:
The Darker Side of Politics

Last Rampage:
The Escape of Gary Tison

On Being Mad or Merely Angry:
John W. Hinckley, Jr., and Other
Dangerous People

On Being Mad
or Merely Angry

JOHN W. HINCKLEY, JR., AND OTHER
DANGEROUS PEOPLE

James W. Clarke

PRINCETON UNIVERSITY PRESS

PRINCETON, NEW JERSEY

Library of Congress Cataloging-in-Publication Data

Clarke, James W., 1937-
On being mad or merely angry : John W. Hinckley, Jr.,
and other dangerous people / James W. Clarke.
p. cm.
Includes bibliographical references.
ISBN 0-691-07852-1
1. Mental illness—Forecasting.
2. Criminals—Identification.
3. Hinckley, John W.—Case studies. I. Title.
RC455.2.F67C53 1990
616.85′82—dc20   89-39421 CIP

This book has been composed in Linotron Palatino

Princeton University Press books are printed on acid-free paper,
and meet the guidelines for permanence and durability of the
Committee on Production Guidelines for Book Longevity
of the Council on Library Resources

Printed in the United States of America by Princeton University Press,
Princeton, New Jersey

1 3 5 7 9 10 8 6 4 2

For Jeanne

————————————————

CONTENTS

PREFACE

QUITE some time ago I began a comprehensive study of American assassins. I was interested not only in the personalities of these unusual men and women but also in the eras and the circumstances in which their attacks occurred. That work, *American Assassins: The Darker Side of Politics*, was published by Princeton University Press in 1982. While the manuscript was in press, John W. Hinckley, Jr., tried to kill President Reagan. Needless to say, I followed the Hinckley case with great interest. In 1985 I began work on this book, using the Hinckley story to illuminate issues that extend beyond this particular young man and his attempt to kill a president.

The book addresses two significant problems in law and mental health: assessing insanity and predicting dangerousness. Both problems also bear directly on the more fundamental issue of responsibility—both individual and social—in American society. Was John W. Hinckley, Jr., truly insane, as the doctors summoned to his defense argued, when he shot President Reagan and three others on March 30, 1981? Or was he simply angry, mentally "disturbed" undoubtedly, but completely aware of what he was about to do, as the doctors who testified for the prosecution insisted? The jury agreed with Hinckley's doctors and attorneys, and he was acquitted. It was the most controversial verdict ever reached in a case involving an attack on an American president.

The book is divided into two sections. The prologue and the first three chapters of Part I take a close look at the reasons for the controversy over Hinckley's sanity, sifting through the details of his troubled life to bring into focus the forces that molded his personality and led to his decision to kill the president. This section concludes in Chapter

Four when, after his acquittal, the question of his sanity shifted to an equally perplexing issue concerning Hinckley's state of mind—his dangerousness.

As the question shifted, so did the opinions of attorneys and doctors. Government attorneys who argued during his trial that Hinckley was sane and responsible now claim that he is a dangerously sick person, an utterly irresponsible threat to the public and himself. Hinckley's doctors and parents, who earlier testified to the severity of his mental and emotional impairment, now insist that his condition has improved and recommend "therapeutic releases" into the community to hasten his recovery and return to society. Thus the lines are drawn between a patient's right to treatment and the government's obligation to ensure the public's safety and welfare. I try to suggest what we, the public, are to make of all this.

In order to do that, in Part II of the book I have placed Hinckley within a broader comparative perspective that takes into account the lives of other dangerous persons, especially previous assassins, would-be assassins, and mass murderers. In *American Assassins* I tried to demonstrate that it was essential to consider the *context* in which violent behavior occurs in order to gain an accurate understanding of motivation. By "context" I mean the array of cultural, political, economic, and social forces that influence our behavior, as well as the immediate situations and circumstances we all confront daily. Oddly enough such influences had been largely ignored in previous studies of American assassins.

In Part II I take this notion of context a step further. Common motivational patterns that Hinckley shares with previous assassins and mass murderers are described in Chapter Five. Chapter Six explains how and why the demographic and clinical indicators employed in actuarial and clinical approaches fail to reveal the critical patterns of behavior that often precede violent acts. These potentially lethal behavioral patterns are described and explained in Chapter

Seven. The chapter closes by describing a new method for identifying and assessing such patterns and, therefore, predicting dangerousness. The broader legal, clinical, and security implications of this research are set forth in Chapter Eight.

On Being Mad or Merely Angry

_____

PROLOGUE

"I REMEMBER waking up early in the morning, seven or eight, and thinking why I couldn't get to sleep," John Hinckley said, recalling the morning of March 30, 1981. He got out of bed, snapped on the *Today* show—or maybe it was *Good Morning, America*, he wasn't sure—on the way to the bathroom. He looked out the window of his Park Central Hotel room, two blocks from the White House, to the busy street below. It was gray and drizzling in Washington that morning, gloomy like his mood. He dressed and, about nine o'clock, left the room he had checked into the night before and walked up K Street to the Crown Bookstore.[1]

Hinckley's tastes in reading ran toward the lives of violent people. Not ordinary husband-kills-wife stuff, but books and articles about people whose crimes had, in some sense, achieved celebrity status for them—mass and serial murderers, skyjackers—and it was hard to name a book he hadn't read about assassins. Occasionally he also read political biographies, most recently books about Ronald Reagan and Edward Kennedy.[a] But John Lennon was his hero. He had read every book and had clipped every article he could find about the slain Beatles star, all of whose albums he had collected since childhood.[2] That morning nothing in the bookstore caught his eye, and he left after half an hour without buying anything. He walked across the street to a McDonald's, where he ordered an Egg McMuffin, and sat there as he ate, contemplating what to do with the rest of his day.[3]

---

[a] Among them were Max Lerner's *Ted and the Kennedy Legend*; *Reagan the Man, the President* by Hedrick Smith, Adam Clymer, Leonard Silk, Robert Lindsey, and Richard Burt; and Doug and Bill Wead's *Reagan in Pursuit of the Presidency—1980*, in addition to numerous articles on both men.

One thing that John Hinckley always had plenty of was time. Lots of time to think or brood, and scheme, often about money. The thing that annoyed him about money was that although there was lots of it in the Hinckley family, he always had a problem prying it loose from his father. Jack Hinckley counted every dollar he gave to his youngest son and was notably disappointed with the way John Jr. had been squandering it for the past seven years. That morning John was down close to the end of the last installment his father had sent; he had somewhere between $130 and $150 left. The question was whether to spend it on a trip to New Haven, where he thought he might kill himself, or whether to remain in Washington where he had been thinking about assassinating Senator Edward Kennedy[b] or, possibly, blasting away in the chambers of the United States Senate, or, if he got lucky, maybe getting a shot at the president. All these ideas had been running through his mind for months.[4]

He was still thinking about the possibilities when he got back to the hotel about 11:30 A.M., bought a *Washington Star*, and took the elevator up to his room. He opened the paper to page A-4, the schedule of congressional activities for that day, scanned it, then turned to the "President's Schedule." President Reagan was scheduled to make a luncheon speech at the Washington Hilton, just up Connecticut Avenue.[5]

While he was considering his options, he decided that in any case he should take a shower and clean up a bit. "It was in the shower," he said, "that I debated whether to detour to the Hilton or go on up to New Haven. I was thinking, should I go over to the Hilton and take my little pistol and see how close I could . . . well, see what the scene was like." He decided to meet the president at the Hilton.[6]

[b] Hinckley had researched the assassinations of Senator Kennedy's brothers, reading books and articles and clipping the latter. See "John W. Hinckley, Jr.," files, FBI File No. 175–601 (1981), pp. H–29, 31, 33.

Why New Haven? In addition to President Reagan, the person who occupied a large place in John Hinckley's thoughts and fantasies was a pretty college freshman at Yale University. Hinckley had been infatuated with the actress Jodie Foster ever since he had seen her in the movie *Taxi Driver*. He had written to her, even talked with her briefly on the telephone a couple of times when he called her Yale dormitory. He had traveled back and forth to New Haven repeatedly, since September, in vain attempts to see her. Disappointed but hardly surprised, he realized that a young woman as appealing as Jodie Foster would be surrounded by attentive males who were better looking than he, more sophisticated, and from families at least as wealthy as his. If he had learned anything during high school and his six years at Texas Tech, it was that he was not a ladies' man. And that was confirmed, once again, in New Haven.

He decided to write a last letter to her anyway. As he sat down at the small desk in his room, he wanted to be sure that he didn't say anything stupid, or something that would offend her. His carefully worded sentiments were something he wanted her to remember. "Dear Jodie," he began. "There is a definite possibility that I will be killed in my attempt to get Reagan. It is for this reason that I am writing you this letter now."[7] Thirty minutes later he closed with "I love you forever, John Hinckley."[8] He dated the letter, marked the time (12:45 P.M.), folded it neatly into an envelope, and placed it in his suitcase.[9]

He then put on his coat and removed a .22 caliber pistol and shook out a couple of handfuls of bullets from boxes in the smaller of his two suitcases. "I had a whole bunch of ammunition with me," he explained later, "cheap ammo, expensive ammo. They all look the same to me."[10]

But they didn't. Hinckley carefully chose the most lethal ammunition, deadly "devastator" bullets, which explode a second time on impact, inside the victim. There were only six devastators among the forty-three bullets he had, and he selected those six when he loaded the pistol. He pock-

eted some extra rounds of regular ammunition in his jacket
along with the gun.[11] Leaving his luggage behind, he ex-
ited the hotel and hailed a cab. As the cab headed north on
busy Connecticut Avenue to the Hilton, about nine minutes away, Hinckley was nervous and very aware that he
should have gone to the bathroom before he left his room.
He asked the driver to stop at the Holiday Inn just short of
his destination. After paying the fare, he dashed inside to
the rest room. When he emerged, he could see the television crews and a crowd gathering outside the T Street side
entrance of the Hilton across the street. He walked over. A
few minutes later the presidential entourage arrived.[12]

Hinckley was impressed when he saw the president, and
excited. "He waved to us," he said, "me and other people
where I was, and the cameramen and all. . . . And when
he waved to us, he was looking right at me and I waved
back. I was kind of startled, but maybe it was just my imagination."[13]

A few minutes after Reagan entered the hotel, Hinckley
walked into the Hilton lobby and sat down to wait for Reagan to finish his speech. A half hour later he got up and
walked back outside. He was having second thoughts.
"Should I? Should I?" he wondered to himself.[14] Then he
decided to set a deadline. "If I was going to have to wait
more than five or ten minutes, I was going to go back to the
hotel. I just wasn't that desperate about it. I just wasn't that
desperate to act that afternoon. . . . Also it was raining and
I wasn't going to stand around in the rain."[15]

Moments later there was a stirring in the lobby as
the president, his speech to thirty-five hundred AFL-CIO
union delegates completed, emerged from the ballroom
surrounded by his Secret Service detail and aides. They
walked briskly through the lobby and outside to the limousine waiting at the curb.

On the sidewalk cameramen and reporters jostled spec-
tators and one another for access to the president. "Press,
press," a reporter said as he tried to elbow Hinckley out of
the way. "No way," Hinckley replied stubbornly, "we
were here first."[16]

"I didn't even see him at first," Hinckley said, "I just saw Secret Service and police. . . . Then I saw him. He was in the midst, of course, waving across the street first, then he turned toward us again, or was in the motion of turning. I never let him get all the way around. That's when I pulled out the gun and started firing."[17]

"I remember an impulse," he said afterward, "put the gun back." But it was too late: "The reporters had already seen the gun."[18] It was 2:25 P.M.

Hinckley emptied his weapon. Six shots in less than three seconds from a crouched position, pistol held professionally with both hands, moving methodically right to left as he tracked the president's movement toward the waiting limousine.[19] Secret Service agents reacted instantly, pushing through the crowd to pounce on Hinckley, who was already in a bystander's grasp, and then wrenching the weapon from his hands and forcing him to the ground.[20]

At the sound of the first shots Secret Service agent Tim McCarthy leaped between the president and the sound of the shots, arms spread wide, providing a human shield. Suddenly he stiffened, then dropped as Hinckley's fourth bullet caught him in the stomach. In another swift movement agent Jerry Parr, who was walking at Reagan's side, grabbed the startled president's shoulders and forced him down behind the opened armored rear door of the limousine only milliseconds before Hinckley's fifth bullet smashed into its bulletproof window.[21] The shot was well aimed. Without the window the bullet would probably have struck the left side of the president's head.[22]

Had it not been for Hinckley's sixth bullet, the president would have been spared entirely due to the quick and courageous actions of McCarthy and Parr. As Reagan was leaning into the limousine, the last bullet hit the rear fender and glanced forward and upward behind the open door, striking the president's left armpit. Reagan groaned when Parr pushed him inside to the floor and dove on top of him. Not yet aware that he had been shot, Reagan attributed the sharp pain that flashed through his chest—"like someone hitting me with a hammer as hard as they could"—to Parr's rough handling. "You sonofabitch, you broke my rib," the president groaned half jokingly as the limousine lurched away from the curb, its tires squealing against the wet pavement.[23]

The scene they left behind was bedlam. Amid the hysterical screams of bystanders, wailing sirens, and shouts of Secret Service agents and police attempting to gain control of the situation, Tim McCarthy lay doubled up on the sidewalk, hands clutching the bullet wound in his stomach; a few feet away police officer Tom Delahanty writhed in agony from a neck wound; next to him lay presidential press secretary Jim Brady, the first to fall, his face flattened against the sidewalk, arms twitching incongruously at his sides, blood trickling into a storm grate from a pea-sized bullet hole over his left eye.[24] Another bullet had narrowly missed the head of presidential aide Michael Deaver before striking a building across the street. Out of six shots it was Hinckley's only clean miss.[c]

First reports of the president's condition, and subsequent White House press releases about his rapid recovery, attempted to conceal the critical nature of his wound. Despite public statements that the president was "A-OK" after having "sailed through surgery" and a hospital spokesman's assurance that he would "be able to make decisions by tomorrow, certainly," persons who saw the president knew differently. Except for an informed snap judgment by Secret Service agent Jerry Parr, the fortuitous presence that afternoon of a very competent trauma team, and two highly skilled thoracic surgeons at George Washington University Hospital, President Reagan would have become the fifth president of the United States to die from an assassin's bullet.

[c] The sequence of Hinckley's shots was as follows: the first hit Brady; the second struck Delahanty; the third almost hit Deaver; the fourth hit McCarthy; the fifth struck the limousine window; the sixth ricocheted off the fender and wounded the president.

Jerry Parr, like Reagan himself, was at first unaware that the president had been hit. In Washington normal procedure in such emergencies is to return directly to the White House, the most secure area in the city. Had that procedure been followed in this instance, Ronald Reagan would surely have died. It was only when Reagan turned to speak that Parr noticed the bright-red oxygenated blood flecking the president's lips and filling the corners of his mouth. He knew at once that the seventy-year-old president had been shot, and that it was life-threatening: a lung wound. Parr immediately ordered the driver, Drew Unrue, to head for the Emergency Room of George Washington University Hospital. Unrue changed routes and radioed ahead to alert the Emergency staff.[25]

By the time they arrived, the color had drained from Reagan's normally ruddy complexion; Parr could tell he was in pain, and then Reagan complained that he was having difficulty breathing. Strangely, a stretcher was not waiting for the stricken president. With Parr's support Reagan tried to walk. He almost made it through the doors. Then he staggered and dropped to one knee. "I can't breathe," he gasped, fear for the first time flickering in his eyes.[26] Parr was afraid they were going to lose him. It was 2:35 P.M.[27]

Within moments the president was wheeled into the trauma room and stripped, and the examination was begun. Doctors found only an entry wound, a gash under his left arm. The bullet was still inside. Reagan was now coughing blood, and his breathing was heavy and irregular. His blood pressure had dropped to seventy-five. Fearing a collapsed lung and other damage to the president's heart or major blood vessels, Dr. Joseph M. Giardano, chief of the trauma team, ordered a chest tube inserted at once and five units of blood to replace the frightening two-and-a-half quarts the president had already lost. Mrs. Reagan arrived and rushed to her husband's side as he was being prepared for surgery. "Honey," he whispered as she bent over him, "I forgot to duck."[28]

As he was wheeled to surgery, the president, still conscious but growing weaker, tried to keep up a good front. "All in all, I'd rather be in Philadelphia," he mumbled through the tubes in his mouth.[29] Then, noticing the masked faces backlit by bright surgical lights suddenly surrounding him in the operating room, he whispered, "Please tell me you're Republicans."[30] Those were the last words he spoke before he lost consciousness.

It was a complicated three-and-a-half hour operation. Dr. Benjamin Aaron, assisted by Dr. Kathleen Cheyney, finally discovered the bullet, "flattened almost as thin as a dime."[31] It had splintered the seventh rib and ricocheted past the heart into the lung. Miraculously the devastator bullet had not exploded inside the president's chest, probably because it had hit the limousine first. A fraction of an inch either way, or a larger caliber bullet, would have been fatal.

Two of Hinckley's other victims, Tom Delahanty and Tim McCarthy, were seriously wounded, but they were expected to survive. There were grave doubts about Jim Brady. Doctors recognized that even if they were able to save Brady's life, the devastator bullet that struck him in the forehead would have caused severe and irreparable damage to his brain. He did survive, but life as the gregarious Jim Brady had known it was over.

Meanwhile, John Hinckley was subdued but responsive enough as he was processed and interrogated in the Central Cell Block of the Metropolitan Police Department.[32] Eddie Meyers, a fourteen-year veteran of the homicide division who looked and talked like a character in an Elmore Leonard novel, sat across from Hinckley, while FBI and Secret Service agents hovered in the background. Meyers had questioned a lot of sleazy people over the years; he knew that he couldn't let what people had done bother him if he wanted information. So when he began to question the chubby, pouting, sandy-haired suspect in front of him, he was friendly.

"I want to hear your side of the story," he said reassuringly. Hinckley had been roughed up a little as he was forced to the pavement after the shooting. The result was a minor scrape on the hand, but it was enough to intimidate a young man unaccustomed to scrapes and bruises. "It's okay," Meyers assured him. "You're perfectly safe here."

Hinckley hesitated before he replied. "I don't know anything about the shooting," he said finally.

"Come on now, John. You must be a Democrat," Meyers said with a smile, hinting at Hinckley's motive.

Hinckley's mouth cracked into a grin. He couldn't help chuckling. No one had joked with him like that in a long, long time.

Later, as Meyers was completing the paperwork on Hinckley's charges, he called to another officer and asked him how to spell "assassinate."

Hinckley looked up with a smirk. "I'll spell it for you," he volunteered before the officer could reply. "A-s-s-a-s-s-i-n-a-t-e."

"Thank you," Meyers replied as he typed the word on the form.

Hinckley smiled again. He seemed to be relaxing.

Hinckley appeared to be in complete control of himself when Dr. William Brownley came in to give him a physical examination. When Brownley finished, noting no abnormalities, an FBI agent who was present during the examination asked Brownley to remove a sample of Hinckley's pubic hair.[33]

"Pubic hair?" Meyers called from across the room in disbelief. "George, for Chrissakes. He didn't fuck Reagan; he shot him."

Hinckley couldn't restrain himself. He doubled over, shaking with laughter. Eddie Meyers was a funny guy. Hinckley liked his sense of humor.[34]

It seemed to everyone who observed John Hinckley those first few hours after his arrest that he was very aware of his situation and in control of himself. Whatever one may think of Eddie Meyer's sense of humor, Hinckley wasn't the only one who laughed there, or later, when the story was recounted, as it often was. Hinckley experienced, and expressed, a normal range of emotions in an appropriate manner throughout the period immediately following his arrest. He was serious when the conversation was serious; and he laughed and traded quips when it wasn't.

He also was quite aware of what he had done and its significance. During his interrogation he had asked Secret Service agent Steve Colo and FBI agent George Chmiel whether his assassination attempt had been taped by television crews on the scene. When Chmiel replied that it was, Hinckley then asked if its showing was going to preempt the Academy Award presentations on television that evening. Both Colo and Chmiel could tell that Hinckley was hoping that it would. He was, they observed, "very concerned about the media exposure affecting other people."[35]

PART I

Chapter One

COMING OF AGE IN DALLAS

WHAT made John Hinckley unusual was his background. The soft cushion of family affluence and the comfortable material life it assured suggested little to be bitter about. But what made him a would-be assassin was his upbringing, comfortable—perhaps too comfortable—and well-intentioned though it was. He was not a marginal person in a sociological sense, not a person one would expect to be criminally inclined. His financially secure upbringing compares only to that of two other political assassins, John Wilkes Booth and Carl Weiss. Hinckley seemed to many to be a wealthy, pampered, suburban child who never grew up, a young man who remained a mama's boy, whining and pouting for his mother's attention and resentful of a father who wanted him to become a man. There is some truth in that, for John Hinckley was a marginal person psychologically—the creation of an anxious, indulgent mother and a well-meaning but demanding and busily distracted father. But like all of us, he was also a product of intangibles. How else could he differ so greatly from an older brother and sister raised in the same environment?

Some of those intangibles were cultural. John Hinckley was a product of the 1970s in America and, one might argue metaphorically without too much exaggeration, *Dallas*—both the city and the television series. The cultural context of that particular era, dominated as it was by the banalities and bogus sophistication of country-club values and hollow solipsistic aspirations, is central to an understanding of John Hinckley. Surrounded all his life by wealthy people with what appeared to be very ordinary talents, John had two goals in life: to be rich, like his father, and to be famous, unlike his father. The goals seemed reasonable at first. After all, his father had preached relent-lessly to all his children—but especially to his timid, appre-hensive younger son—that there were no limits to what a man could achieve in America if he was willing to apply himself and work. And, of course, Jack Hinckley was the self-satisfied, living example of his own tedious, repeti-tious sermons.

But nothing John ever did pleased his father—at least, he never heard his father say he was pleased. As a child John resented him; as he grew older that resentment turned to hatred. That situation—that absence of a positive male fig-ure in his life—was a major reason why, at the age of twenty-five, John Hinckley was trying still to decide *who* he was and, in the process, get back at the father he could never please.

Mom and Dad

John W. Hinckley, Jr., was born on May 29, 1955, in Ard-more, Oklahoma, the third and youngest child of his par-ents, Jack and Jo Ann. Like his older brother and sister, Scott and Diane, he was born healthy, attractive, and intel-ligent into a solidly middle-class Midwestern family with traditional moral and religious values. There were loving grandparents, family vacations, pets to cuddle, new toys to look forward to every Christmas, and a mother who was *always* there. It seemed all the elements were present for little John Jr. to have a comfortable and happy childhood. On the surface the Hinckleys seemed like one of those fam-ilies in the television sitcoms that were popular at that time—shows like *Leave It to Beaver*, *Ozzie and Harriet*, or, more to the point of this chapter, *Father Knows Best*. But the television families solve their problems and leave everyone smiling within a half hour. In the Hinckleys' case, on the contrary, the problem that developed continued to grow over the years to tragic proportions.

Jo Ann Hinckley (until 1981 she was called Jodie by her family and friends) was the typical housewife of that era, baking cookies, washing and ironing, keeping the house spotless. Each chore was carefully planned and scheduled, just like the three meals she prepared for her family every day. And then, of course, she spent a good bit of time in the family station wagon, shopping and shuttling the kids around to dental appointments and keeping up with all their various carefully arranged activities. Everything had a time and place in a life devotedly structured around her husband and children. In the afternoons, when the kids were in school or out playing, she would have some time alone to watch the game shows she enjoyed. But even then she usually ironed. "How many shirts I pressed in thirty-four years of marriage," she said, looking back over those years, "and every one with pride."[1] She was exactly the kind of mother companies like Procter and Gamble and Lever Brothers wanted to portray in their commercials.

But her husband wasn't quite the traditional father—at least not in the mellow, approachable way fathers were portrayed in those television shows. Despite the best intentions, Jack was too busy to be the kind of father who came home on time for meals and spent his evenings with the family, smoking a pipe or puttering around with a hobby in the basement. Jack Hinckley was a driving, ambitious, self-made man, a man for whom time meant money, not refinishing antiques or showing his sons how to build bird houses as Fred MacMurray did in "My Three Sons." It was quicker to buy those things. Time and money. Neither was meant to be squandered; that was one lesson he tried to teach his three children.

Jack Hinckley had always had goals and been in a rush to reach them. In 1942, a year before he was to graduate from high school, he was accepted into an accelerated naval officer training program at the University of Oklahoma. Within three years he had completed both high school and college, earning a degree in mechanical engineering and an ensign's commission. Even in an accelerated, academically demanding program he found time to earn spending money by playing drums in a dance band, was active in several honor societies, and managed to get himself elected vice-president of his class. By the time he was twenty-one he had completed his education, served his country as a naval officer, gotten himself a job with Carter Oil Company when he was discharged, and, best of all, on Christmas Eve that same year, married a pretty blonde freshman who thought she was the luckiest young lady in the world when he proposed. It was 1946.[2]

Where did he get that drive? It wasn't from his father, as one might expect. He was too young when his father died to remember him. Jack was raised by a stepfather, a man his mother married when Jack was eight years old. A reserved, distant man, he spoke rarely and then usually to express displeasure. On those rare occasions when Jack mentions his stepfather, it is always by name, Kib Brooks, without any adjectives one way or another.[3]

Jack adored his mother. But she was a sickly woman who kept things to herself, suffering for years with cancer and never telling her family. Thus it was not until shortly before her death that Jack and his sister finally understood what was wrong all those years she had silently endured the pain.[4]

Those silences and that uncertainty, however, didn't seem to draw Jack and his older sister, Avilla, together, as sometimes happens. Instead, an intense rivalry characterized their relationship. According to Jack, he usually lost. "Avilla outshone me at everything," he said, adding that she was a "straight-A student"; it didn't help that she was also "a tall, blonde beauty."[5] Perhaps it was this chilly mix of influences as Jack Hinckley was growing up that accounts for his independence, his insistence on self-reliance, and the consuming ambition for success that shaped the lives of his own children.

MOVING UP IN THE WORLD

To get ahead, Jack believed, you had to be willing to move. And the Hinckleys did, from drilling site to drilling site, fourteen times in the first five years of their marriage. After

Scott was born in 1950 they decided to settle down in Ardmore, Oklahoma, where they had lived for two years, to
raise a family. Diane was born three years later, in 1953;
John's birth followed in 1955. But it wasn't just the moves
that put strains on the family, it was Jack's absences. "If
hard work could provide our children with a good home
and a decent education," he said, "they were going to have
them."[6] But all that hard work took its toll as his children
went to bed at night and got up in the morning too often
without him. And it was hard on both him and Jo Ann.
"Many months I'd see Jo Ann only occasionally, sleeping
most nights in my car at a drilling site, longing to be with
her. I was doing it all for Jo Ann, I believed, to earn the
good life post-war America held out to those who were
willing to work."[7]

The next year, 1956, was their tenth anniversary. After
ten years of working for someone else, Jack Hinckley was
restless and dissatisfied. He decided to strike out on his
own, hoping to make more money and have more control
over his time so he could be with his family more. But it
didn't work out that way. The good life Jack sought proved
to be more elusive than he planned. It was rough as he
tried to build a business as an independent "petroleum
consultant." He still worked night and day, now trying to
establish contacts instead of supervising drilling sites, but
few sought his services at the tiny office in Ardmore. After
two frustrating years of moonlighting—building storm
shelters and swimming pools—to pay the bills, he decided
to give up. He had to make a change if he was going to
make the kind of money he intended to make, and Ardmore wasn't the place to do it. Denver and Dallas were
where the money was in the petroleum industry. By the
time the Hinckleys moved to Dallas in 1958 Jack admitted
that he had been so wrapped up in business, he barely
knew his three-year-old son.[8]

Jo Ann was apprehensive about the move, but Jack always made the big decisions, so she went along with this
one as she had all the others. But it was different this time.
She liked Ardmore and its small-town ways, especially

with her husband away so much. Folksy and familiar, Ardmore seemed like home after ten years. She had her friends, her church; all the little routines of daily life were set and familiar. The town provided the kind of environment she wanted her children to grow up in. Ardmore seemed like a lot to give up for a big city in Texas that was twice as far from her mother in Oklahoma City.

The move to Dallas proved to be more difficult for Jo Ann than anyone imagined it would be. She was terrified by the size, pace, and impersonality of the city. She hated the rented house they moved into but was afraid to leave it. The good shopping she was promised became a nightmare; each trip to even a grocery store became an ordeal, as she fought the panic that swelled up and caught in her throat when she confronted strange people and strange situations. Sometimes overwhelmed, she would grab the children and rush out of the store, leaving her purchases behind.[9]

Jack wasn't very understanding about what he considered Jo Ann's "imaginary" problems. He was working long hours to establish himself in a new job, and was tired and distracted—or "up-tight," as he described it—much of the time when he was at home. With all the pressures and problems he had to contend with each day, it was hard to sympathize with someone who couldn't go to a supermarket once a week without ending up in hysterics. Each time one of her anxiety attacks occurred it would release a stable of emotions in Jack: alarm would lead but fade quickly as impatience closed in, only to be overtaken by disgust. Jo Ann could tell from his expressions and suggestions—such as "getting away from the kids for a few hours"—that her husband had little appreciation of what she was going through.[10] She spent a lot of time just crying. The children didn't understand, but Scott and Diane were in school and gone most of the day. It was the youngest, John, who was there alone with her all day long, absorbing her fears and anxieties—and resenting his father's disdain during those rare evenings when he was home.

It was during this difficult period that Jo Ann's mother came to visit and help with the children. On a trip to the supermarket, Jo Ann said, "Mother glanced down at the small towheaded boy clinging to me. . . . John was clutching my skirt in his little fist as though life depended on it." Feeling a need to explain the child's fearfulness, she told her mother that it was because he was unfamiliar with the store. But she also realized that John alone of her three children seemed overwhelmed by such fears, and he carried them with him as he grew older.[11]

Buying a new house in the attractive University Park section of the city marked the first sign of improvement in Jo Ann's outlook. After finally seeing a doctor who convinced her that there was no organic basis to her fears, she gradually found it within herself to get out of the house more. She became involved in activities at the children's school and the Episcopal church, and eventually she joined a bridge club. The change came as a big relief to Jack. The first year in Dallas had been rough on everyone, but everyone seemed to have weathered it all right, except John.[12]

The transition had been easiest for Scott and Diane. Both were doing fine: they had lots of friends, they got good grades in school. Even John seemed to be giving up his clinging ways, to a degree, after he started school. In the more structured primary grades he seemed to be a fairly typical child—with no special talents, no special problems—who played basketball and football in elementary school and had an ordinary range of friends and other activities.

But John was too quiet. He rarely initiated conversations. If his birthday parties were boisterous, as his father remembered them, it was because of the other children. Jo Ann could hardly miss that he was uncomfortable away from home. She had to urge him to seek out his playmates or arrange meetings for him herself. If children came to see him, he played with them; if not, he was content to remain home, near his mother. He was very different from his brother and sister, she realized, but she decided that it was probably just shyness, one of those stages children go through. In fact, she claimed that it was a relief to have a child "who wasn't," as she put it, "especially adventuresome. . . . with two lively older children to keep track of, I was grateful that my third was such a stay-at-home."[13]

But he remained a stay-at-home. When a boy approaches adolescence and such patterns of dependency don't begin to change, when he doesn't begin to venture out with friends his own age, it becomes a concern. And the Hinckleys *were* concerned, not only for John, but also for themselves: the strains that were always there in their marriage were exacerbated by John's continuing dependence on his mother.

Perhaps it was the onset of adolescence, when other children are beginning to assert their independence, that made him feel different, that made him feel he didn't fit in. It was all right when his mother planned his birthday parties and invited friends in to play. But he was too old to be thought of as a shy little boy now; his peers probably began to find such motherly intrusions odd and perhaps even offensive.

His withdrawal, although gradual, was completed within two years. He dropped out of sports, the primary source of his social activity up until that time. His move to the sidelines became a metaphor for the rest of his life. The first sign was his decision not to play; he wanted to be a "team manager" instead. Maybe it was the stiffer competition at that age. Disparities in ability become more noticeable in adolescence as some boys develop their coordination more quickly than others and performance is evaluated less benignly than it is among younger boys. The social pressures are no longer there to conceal disappointment in another's performance under a facade of uncaring good sportsmanship. Ridicule is more readily expressed in words and looks by everyone involved: players, coaches, and parents. Or it could have been the embarrassment of the showers and locker-room vulgarity after the games. Whatever it was, after a year or so he dropped sports altogether.

There can be little doubt that moving again hastened his move to the sidelines of life. It was 1966 when Jack decided that it was time to relocate—this time merely across town, to a fancier neighborhood and a stately old house on Beverly Drive in Highland Park, a Dallas suburb a step or two above their University Park address. It was a move in keeping with Jack's decision a year before to borrow money to establish his own business as an independent oil producer. "I was forty that year," he said, explaining the decision, "the age at which ambition suddenly demands a time-table."[14]

It was also a move into the country-club society of Dallas, where, more than anything else, money and its adornments determine an individual's importance. It was that kind of respectability that Jack had worked all his life to attain. It must have felt good to write "President, Vanderbilt Energy Corporation" on the membership application.

What the move meant for his eleven-year-old son was another matter: the loss of the few friends he had, a familiar school and way of life. John's obvious unhappiness about something Jack felt so good about made him angry. He had been through all that once before, and he was in no mood for a rerun. He had neither the time nor the patience to deal with any more "imaginary" problems—either Jo Ann's or John's. "It was inconceivable to me," Jack said, "that he could be unhappy. Why, our kids had every-thing—a yard to play in, a TV set in the living room, water-skiing on weekends with our outboard motorboat. We were the family whose American dream had come true."[15]

After the move to Highland Park John Hinckley rarely had a sustained conversation with anyone except his mother. When his few friends started to date, John was left out. He never dated in high school.[16] Most of the time he just stayed in his room, usually playing Beatles records. And because of Jack's growing resentment toward the son who was so unlike himself, John's cherished conversations with his mother had to be guarded, had to occur only when Jack wasn't around. It was sad, but the knowledge of the now furtive nature of their relationship made both John and his mother feel uncomfortable. It was as if they were doing something wrong, and John's resentment of his father deepened because of it.

That wasn't the only thing about his father's domineering presence that he resented. On those rare occasions when John did try to talk to his father, it always ended the same way: Jack talked and John listened to why *he* was wrong. There just had never been much communication between Jack and his youngest child. Sure, there had been attempts to bring them closer when John was younger, but they were all too contrived. There was never any spontaneously expressed warmth between the two. The "Indian Guides" experience at the YMCA seems to have been typical of such efforts. Indian Guides was, as Jack unenthusiastically described it, "a group of eight or ten fathers and sons sitting cross-legged for several hours each month, wearing feathered headdresses and solemnly weaving belts out of leather." It was primarily the conversations with the other fathers that made the sessions bearable, Jack admitted.[17] There were also a couple of trips the two had taken together—John doesn't remember much about them—when he was a little boy. But it seems those Indian Guides sessions were about as close as Jack ever got to spending any significant time alone with his younger son. As they both grew older, the distance between them widened. John was just a little boy the last time his father hugged him, as far as Jack could remember. After that time not even a pat on the shoulder passed from father to son.[18]

Jack recalled having been easier on John than on Scott when they were growing up. "I'd been far more demanding with Scott," he said, "scolded him, spanked him a lot more often. . . . I hadn't been half as tough on John. . . . About the only thing I ever recall reprimanding John for was playing his phonograph too loud."[19]

Instead of spankings and reprimands there was ridicule—invidious comparisons between John and his popular older brother and sister—and disdain. As Jack has said, "John's indifference to anything mechanical was a constant source of amazement to Scott and me, both mechanical engineers."[20] In contrast to the accomplishments of Scott and Diane there was little that John Hinckley ever did that his father appreciated or approved of. For example, John's interest in music and poetry he dismissed as evidence of John's "lack of any concept of what it took to get ahead in the real world."[21]

His mother could see what was happening, and she felt sorry for her son. It was a dilemma. On the one hand, she wanted John to develop some initiative and direction in his life as badly as her husband did. But possibly because of Jack's scathing ridicule, the way he often belittled the boy, she had no choice but to defend him. She knew he had to change, but she could also empathize with his fears and timidity—and, recalling the difficult period he shared with her that first year in Dallas and the way she pampered him after that, she may have felt somewhat responsible.

But that didn't make the situation now any easier to contend with. Arguments occurred regularly; every meal together became a reason for anxiety. When the three of them sat down to eat, either the meal was silent or an argument developed before they were finished. When Jack accused her of pampering John, she knew it was true, but what else could she do in the face of Jack's overbearing manner and constant badgering? Why couldn't he see that his ridicule was undermining the very self-reliance he wanted John to develop?

But lacking a clear purpose in her own life at this stage, she was unable to counter the criticism or to suggest an acceptable alternative. Instead she tried to compensate for Jack's incapacity to give John love and understanding. But it was difficult. When Jack was around, he obviously resented any attention she gave their boy, so to keep peace between them she had to sneak. It was only when Jack was away that she could express her love for her youngest child; otherwise she was forced to play Jack's game or endure a sleepless night arguing. She was well aware that Jack considered his son an unwelcome intruder in the house, an annoying rival for her attention. At times she felt she was being forced by both her husband and her son to make a choice: one or the other.

THE EXILE

The normal pattern for a child growing up is to find, usually during adolescence, that friends are more interesting and fun to be with than parents. Parents become less important to his emotional needs. It is a critical period of development, according to psychologists, during which the child not only establishes his sexual identity, both physically and emotionally, but also redefines his relationship to authority. The child does this, in large part, by asserting his independence from his parents and assuming greater responsibility for his own welfare. The process by which the child "cuts the apron strings," or distances himself from the parents, is formalized when he becomes self-supporting and moves out of the house. Parents may encourage and facilitate the process, but, as a rule, it is the child—and not they—who makes this decision. If the process is reversed, it can be traumatic, conveying a sense of banishment and arousing feelings of ultimate rejection in the child. So it was with John Hinckley.

By the time Hinckley graduated from high school in 1973 his sulking dependence on his mother had become not only an embarrassment, especially to his father, but also the source of great strains on his parents' marriage. The Hinckleys were in their mid-forties, at a stage in their own lives when they were ready to put the responsibilities of child rearing behind them, to enjoy the freedom to pursue interests apart from their children. But John showed no evidence of having a plan to leave home. Jack was ashamed of him. In contrast to Scott and Diane, John was rarely mentioned to friends and even less often introduced to visitors.[22] Even his mother was becoming weary of his presence and the strains it caused.

Characteristically blunt, Jack said that he wanted John out of the house. Fortunately there was a nice antiseptic way to accomplish that purpose. He made it clear that John, like it or not, was going to college. Both Scott and Diane had done so, and there was no reason why he shouldn't as well. But John didn't want to go. As bored and as unhappy as he seemed to be moping around the house or sitting alone in his room, he didn't want to leave home— or, more to the point, his mother.

After several meetings with a high school guidance counselor Jack decided that Texas Tech would be appropriate and that John would major in business.[23] As with most of his father's views, John didn't agree. But this time, for a change, he said so. He didn't see the need for college, he protested, adding that he didn't want to leave Dallas; moreover, he made it clear that he definitely did not want to study business. His interests were music and literature, he insisted.

It didn't matter. Jack, who had spent the last several years traveling back and forth to New York to borrow investment capital for the oil exploration company he had founded, scoffed at the thought. John, he maintained, needed to study something "realistic" that would prepare him to earn a living. "A liberal arts degree," he said, "wouldn't mean very much at a job interview."[24]

In the meantime, unhappy with what life had become in Dallas—due, in large part, to John and the strains his presence was putting on the marriage—Jack decided that he and Jo Ann needed a change. Scott had finished at Vanderbilt University and was working for an oil company in Indonesia; Diane was in her last year at Southern Methodist, planning to marry soon; and his company, Vanderbilt Energy Corporation, could be run just as well from Denver. There was nothing but his wife's objections to hold them in Dallas. In September 1973, a month after they had packed their reluctant son off to Texas Tech in Lubbock, the Hinckleys moved to Evergreen, Colorado, a wealthy suburb in the Denver foothills. It was to be another stab at a new life for Jack and Jo Ann, an attempt to sweeten a marriage that was going sour.[25] For their youngest child their move meant that on top of being separated from his mother, he no longer even had a home to return to in Dallas. It was exile, and John Hinckley resented it deeply.

Chapter Two

THE ROAD TO RUIN

IT WAS during the seven lonely years of what he considered to be his exile that John Hinckley's social withdrawal became so complete that he gradually withdrew psychologically into a world of his own making, losing his capacity to think clearly or rationally in the midsts of his fantasies—or so an impressive battery of psychiatrists for the defense testified at his trial. While it is not my intent in this chapter to catalogue every aspect of Hinckley's lonely life during this period, there are several episodes that stand as mileposts on Hinckley's road to ruin.

FROM LUBBOCK TO HOLLYWOOD

John Hinckley remained the same friendless person at Texas Tech in the fall of 1973 that he had been during high school. Emotionally he had relied completely on his mother. In Lubbock he no longer had her stabilizing influence to check his drifting existence. And drift he did, without social connections or control, trying to find himself. For the next seven years John Hinckley dropped in and out of school, moving from apartment to apartment, managing to complete only three years of credit by 1980 when he finally dropped out and, much to his parents' dismay, returned home to stay.

He carried the same emotional baggage he had left Dallas with, and he had picked up more along the way. He had become a young man only a mother could love, and even she found it difficult to have him around. His self-absorption drained her emotions and energy and left her depressed. He still had no clear sense of his own identity or what to do with his life, and the ulcerated relationship with his father had gotten worse with each passing, unproductive year, as contempt gradually replaced shame in his father's feelings toward him.

His mother was in despair, not knowing what to do about the worsening situation. The lovely native-stone-and-timber house in the Colorado foothills made no difference. The expansive views of the Rockies, the huge fireplace, the crystal chandelier hanging from the cathedral ceiling—nothing made a difference. When John was home, it was even worse than it had been in Dallas; the new house—which was designed to lift their moods, to focus their attention on the mountains beyond—became a claustrophobic temple of doom. She and her husband found themselves spending as little time there as possible.

The whole time Hinckley had been in college he continued to demand their attention. He was never out of their minds. There were letters and phone calls, almost always about problems. There were two persistent themes, health and money. He complained about one ailment after another with symptoms like "pressure" in his throat or a "rocking" feeling in his head. Then his weight would balloon up, at one point to 230 pounds, making him look lumpy, ugly, and, somehow, small. Physical examinations would reveal no cause or explanation for his complaints. Drugs would be prescribed, usually tranquilizers like the Surmontil a Lubbock doctor prescribed, to calm his anxieties about his health. Away from home he continued, one way or another, to remind his parents—his mother especially—of what *they* were doing to him.

In April 1976, for example, John startled his parents with this note:

Dear Mom and Dad,
    By the time you receive this letter, I will no longer be in Lubbock. I have dropped out of school. I know you'll never understand, but I'm too miserable here to take it any longer. I honestly won't blame you if you get mad and cut me

off. . . . I'm sorry I'm doing this to you. . . . I only hope someday I can make you proud of me.

It was signed, "Love, John."[1]

There had been no warning. There was no hint of where he had gone. No one in Lubbock knew anything more than that he had moved out of his apartment and dropped out of school. His parents worried—which is, of course, what he hoped they would do—but, interestingly, they made no effort to locate him other than asking people in Lubbock. A month went by before a Mother's Day card arrived with a Los Angeles postmark.

In the letter he enclosed with it, John told his parents that he was in Hollywood "within easy walking distance of about 30 of the most famous music publishers in the world . . . trying to sell some of my songs." He went on to say that he hoped they were not "too disappointed in me for dropping out of school," adding that "for the first time in years I am happy." In closing he said that he hoped his newfound happiness would make them "at least tolerant" of his actions.[2]

John Hinckley had loved the Beatles from the moment he first heard their music in the early 1960s when he was eight years old. Two years later his parents had bought him an electric guitar, which he learned to play as he sat in his room surrounded by photographs and magazine articles about the popular group and especially his idol, John Lennon. If he could have had one wish, it probably would have been to become someone like John Lennon. In this context the trip to Hollywood may be understood as an attempt to make that wish come true. Nothing ventured, nothing gained, as his father had said so many times. This was to be John Hinckley's first venture on his own.

But like most of the many young people who have traveled to Hollywood for similar reasons, he failed in his plan. A couple of weeks after Mother's Day, his parents received another letter, this one announcing that things had taken a sharp turn for the worse: he had been burglarized. The letter was oozing with self-pity expressed in passages like this: "Your son, for the past 2½ weeks, has had to walk up to strangers and ask them for spare change, so I can eat. Although I am physically ravaged, my spirit has not *yet* been broken." Then he got to the point: "You don't know how grateful I would be if you could give me limited financial support and a great deal of moral support during this period." The message was sharpened in the next paragraph with "please send cash." Then he applied a rich layer of guilt as he closed: "On the other hand, if you feel that being robbed is just what I deserve for the way I've acted, I'll try to understand."

It worked, as it always had. After a couple of paragraphs of that, his mother was weeping and Jack had dashed off to wire money, concerned about his son, but less so than about the tears this troublesome boy had brought to his mother's eyes.[3]

A few days later, when John called to say he had received the money, they learned that he had sold the Camaro his father had bought him only months before and had used the money for the trip. Jack was livid at first but then took comfort in subsequent letters they received which suggested that John was at least looking for work. "Please keep in mind," he wrote, "the only reason I'm out here in Hollywood is to try and attain some success with my music and this could be the golden opportunity I've been looking for." Let's hope and pray, Jack probably thought as he wired more money with a congratulatory note.[4]

Then in July they received more good news: John had a "contact" at United Artists who was looking at his music and, at long last, he had a girlfriend, an aspiring young actress named Lynn Collins whom he said he had met in a Hollywood laundromat. In letters and phone calls that followed he described restaurants where he and Lynn had dined and trips they had taken together to Malibu Beach. Her family, he hinted, was quite wealthy; "they're behind her all the way," he added meaningfully. "Write soon."

And his encouraged parents did, with additional money accompanying virtually every letter.[5]

The whole story was a hoax, of course. It was concocted solely as a means to keep the dollars flowing west from Evergreen. He knew there were three things his parents wanted him to do more than anything: leave home, succeed at something, and find a girlfriend. So he strung the story out as long as he could. But by the end of the summer he had tired of L.A. and needed a reason to leave. His parents received the inevitable tale of woe in September when another letter arrived. It began with how he had been stuck in an elevator, then got worse as he moved through "severe eye sting attacks" that forced him to leave his job, being dumped by United Artists, a near mugging, and finally, worst of all, his breakup with Lynn. "Now if you'll excuse me," he concluded, "I think I'm going to go and kill myself. (Just kidding . . . I think)."[6] His parents fell for it. A few days later he was back in Evergreen.

FINDING A JOB

It was to remain a familiar pattern. John was like a boomerang cast from his parents' home: Lubbock and back; Los Angeles and back; Dallas and back; the traveling not only continued, it accelerated as John Hinckley's search for himself became more frantic. As the stress continued to increase, so did his ailments. When he wasn't home there were more phone calls, more complaints about headaches, earaches, backaches, colds, chest pains, pains in his arms and legs, things caught in his throat, insomnia—anything, it seemed, to keep his parents off balance.

Jack was exasperated. During the periods when John was back in Evergreen Jack insisted that he look for work. He didn't want him lounging around the house or sulking in his room, listening to records and munching his mother's cookies, as he was inclined to do. When the suggestion was made, John countered with yet another problem: he was afraid to drive in Denver traffic. When Jo Ann quietly reminded her husband that their son was also afraid to drive at night, Jack just shook his head.[7]

Afraid to drive in traffic? And at night? It was hard to accept. What could any father say about a grown son like that? When Jack was John's age, he was serving as a naval officer—in a war! But much to her husband's dismay Jo Ann agreed to chauffeur her son back and forth—an hour each way—between Evergreen and Denver for job interviews.

Eventually someone hired this unimpressive young man whose mother waited outside during the interviews. The job was as a busboy at a nightclub. It wasn't much, but he had never worked at anything other than menial jobs, and never for very long. Since he was afraid to drive at night, his father insisted that he take a motel room across the street from the nightclub to spare Jo Ann—not to mention to get him out of the house. Even so, she dropped by regularly to keep her chubby son supplied in cookies and casseroles, feeling bad every time she looked at his only companion in the dingy room, a small black and white TV.[8]

After five months of clearing tables and sweeping floors he quit, or was fired. It isn't certain which. It was the longest he had worked at any job and the closest he had ever come to supporting himself. He then managed to convince his parents that he deserved another chance with his music and a trip to Los Angeles to pursue it. Two weeks later he called collect from Los Angeles to ask for plane fare back home. Then it was back to Texas Tech with a new major in liberal arts that his exasperated father himself had suggested.

The situation was becoming unbearable for his parents. In the midst of this turmoil Jack, in desperation, sought solace in religion, turning over, as he put it, "my life, my possessions, my family," to God. Religion became a temporary escape from the problems at home as he began to travel regularly to Africa, Central America, and Miami (Haitian refugees), working on the worldwide Christian relief projects of the Christian Aid Mission and another organization called World Vision.[9] When he wasn't away on such projects, he and Jo Ann traveled from one place to another: Europe, the Bahamas, a golf condominium they had purchased in Southern California, a dude ranch in Arizona—anywhere to have some time to themselves away from their son. Mother, father, and son careened from one place to another in a desperate Oedipal contest of wills and emotions that they didn't seem to understand, a contest that they all would ultimately lose.

FROM LUBBOCK TO NEW HAVEN

In reality it was not the fictitious Lynn who occupied John Hinckley's thoughts and imagination, although she was resurrected briefly in 1979 when he again needed money from his parents. It was a real young actress who had caught his eye on that trip to California in 1976. Jodie Foster played the role of Iris, a child prostitute in a film he saw there, *Taxi Driver*. Hinckley thought she was beautiful, the most attractive female he had ever seen. She became his fantasy and, ultimately, his obsession. He wrote songs and poems about her and to her. His thoughts were sweet and endearing, never lewd or explicitly sexual, as one might expect of fantasies about a prostitute. There was never more than a hint of sexuality in the words of this sexually repressed young man.[10]

Hinckley also found the main character in the film appealing, a cabdriver, Travis Bickle. Bickle, played by Robert DeNiro, is a lonely, angry man who tries to kill a political candidate and, in the final scenes of the film, becomes a mass killer as he rescues Iris from her pimps. In his search for identity Hinckley, like many younger children whose heroes change with age and the resonance of impressions made by certain screen or sports heroes, gradually began to shift from the Beatles to this fictional role model. Perhaps it was because of the disappointments in Hollywood and the realization that a career like John Lennon's was out of reach that his interests changed. As he began to share Travis Bickle's love for the underage prostitute, John Hinckley began to imitate other features of Bickle's life, including his tastes in clothing (an army fatigue jacket and jeans) as well as the handguns he fondled in his lonely room, staring blankly at a flickering television screen. In the summer of 1979 Hinckley bought his first handgun at the Galaxy Pawn Shop in Lubbock and began practicing with it.[11]

It was also at about this time that Hinckley's curiosity about desperate men with violent pasts and reputations came to full bloom. He first began to read about the Nazi movement for that reason, but his interest soon focused on the lives of violent individuals, people who had been involved in spectacular crimes where weapons had played a part. Hijackers, kidnappers, serial killers, mass murderers, and assassins became his heroes as he collected books and articles about them, probably seeking some vicarious release from the frustration and anger that was building within himself.[a]

[a] Among the many books Hinckley collected and read were: *The Myth of the Six Million* (an anonymously written pro-Nazi book that argues that the Holocaust did not occur); *Welcome to Xanadu* (a fictional account of a kidnapper who eventually commits suicide); *The Fox Is Crazy Too* (a true story about a skyjacker); *The Fan* (a novel about a man who stalks and kills an actress); *Fade to Black* (a novel about a serial killer); *The Boston Strangler* (a true account of a serial killer); Priscilla McMillan's, *Marina and Lee* (a true story about the Oswalds); Robert Blair Kaiser's *R.F.K. Must Die!* (a true account of the trial of Sirhan Sirhan); *Starkweather* (a factual account of the murderous rampage of Charles Starkweather and his teenage girlfriend); and Arthur Bremer's *An Assassin's Diary*. Hinckley had also written a college term paper that he had plagiarized from *Starkweather*.

Among the articles he had clipped were a number about the Wallace shooting: "Wallace Shot," *Dallas Morning News*, April 16, 1972, as well as articles from *Time* and *Life* published the week of the shooting. Several articles were about mass killer Charles Whitman. Hinckley also had a bibliography of published materials on President Kennedy's assassination.

See "John W. Hinckley, Jr.," files, FBI File No. 175–601 (1981), "Evidence from Evergreen, Colorado." See also United States v. John W. Hinckley, Jr., Cr. No. 81–3–306 (1981), testimony of Dr. David Bear, pp. 3847, 3878–3884, and testimony of Dr. Park Dietz, pp. 6546–6561, 6626–6627, 6629, and 6946.

By September 1980 Hinckley had seen the movie *Taxi Driver* many of the fifteen times he claims that he ultimately saw it. It wasn't the violence in the film that intrigued him primarily, although he found it fascinating; it was Iris—a beautiful, sexy little girl. Her childlike vulnerability was irresistible to this immature young man whose emotional development had never progressed beyond adolescence. It was the compelling mix of sensuality and innocence that Iris conveyed on the screen that got him. She was everything he wanted.

But how could he meet her? For four years he had fantasized about Jodie Foster—not Iris—collecting photographs and magazine articles about her. It was in May 1980 that he read in *People* magazine that she would begin attending Yale University that September. For the rest of the summer he thought about how he might use that opportunity to meet her. He knew that a date with Jodie Foster was a long shot, but he decided to try anyway. For once he would invoke some of the well-known Hinckley initiative and determination that his father had chided him for lacking for as long as he could remember. If old demanding, self-satisfied Jack only knew what he was up to now, he probably thought. What would his father and mother think if he were to bring a famous movie star home to meet the family? Would they be impressed? Would it be something that Scott—Vanderbilt, engineering degree, all that—would ever come close to doing? Just the thought probably brought a smile to his lips. Sweet revenge.

But first he needed an excuse to get to New Haven. He couldn't just tell his parents he wanted to go there to meet Jodie Foster. He could imagine what his father would say about that. Even his mother would think he was crazy. As he housesat while his parents were in Europe that summer, he thought of a scheme. What if he said he wanted to study something at Yale? Jack might spring for that. He had recently relented on his insistence that John study business; nearly seven frustrating years had finally worn down his resolve. Now John knew that his father didn't care what he studied—or did—as long as it was something, and away from home. Yale was away from home, but he would need to pry some money out of his parents. When they returned from Europe, he announced that he wanted to attend a writer's workshop that was being held at Yale University in September.

For some time Hinckley had resented the fact that his father had refused to let him have access to a trust account that Jack had established for each of the children. Scott and Diane had been given theirs, but Jack had withheld his, claiming correctly that John had not yet learned to manage money responsibly. Now John wanted his share to cover his expenses in New Haven. As further evidence of his willingness to do anything he could to help resolve his son's problems, Jack agreed. He gave John a check for $3,600 drawn from John's trust account to use in New Haven. The only condition was that he then return to Texas Tech to complete his degree.[12] The writer's workshop ploy was yet another shrewd move on Hinckley's part to get what he wanted.

His mother was excited and hopeful when John asked her to drive him into Denver to spend a day shopping together. He wanted her to help him select a new wardrobe for the trip. She saw nothing unusual in such a request from a young man of twenty-five, just as she saw nothing particularly odd about his fears of city traffic and driving after dark.[13]

Hinckley, of course, had no intention of attending a workshop on anything at Yale. He arrived in New Haven on September 17, 1980, for the sole purpose of meeting Jodie Foster at her Yale dormitory. Within hours of arriving he called and talked briefly with her on the telephone. And he kept calling for the next three days. But after a few short phone conversations, she refused to talk to him.[14] Frustrated, he went to the campus in an attempt to see her as she walked back and forth to classes. When he did, however, he found himself too apprehensive to approach her. "Just basically shyness," he explained later. "I mean she was a pretty famous movie star and there I was, Mr. Insignificant himself."[15]

Hinckley was also sensitive to the looks and sneers that followed as male students began to notice him loitering around the women's dormitory. "Mr. Toxic Shock," they chuckled behind the back of this obviously out-of-place young man.

Jodie Foster and her roommate had at first treated him with polite indifference on the phone; after all, he wasn't the first young man at Yale to pester a pretty student. But both made it clear that Jodie wanted him to leave her alone, especially after the tone of the "love notes" he left for her at the dorm became a little too insistent. At about this time, too, the FBI had warned Foster of an anonymous kidnap threat they had received. John Hinckley, it was established later, had made the threat.[16]

After three unrewarding days of courtship John called his mother to say that he didn't like the workshop (no explanation), New Haven (dirty, industrial, and too expensive), or the students (sloppy and unfriendly). He wanted to come home. Disgusted, his father didn't want to be there if he did. The next day Jack left for a World Vision meeting in California.[17]

Sensing the consternation at home, John remained in New Haven for another day skulking around the Yale campus, trying to sneak glimpses of Foster. On September 22 the phone rang in Evergreen. When his mother answered it, it was John calling to ask her to pick him up at the Denver airport. He told her that he was on his way back to Lubbock to close out his checking account there. He was depressed, he said, and he didn't want to go back to Texas Tech. He went on to say that he had also quit the writer's program and needed a couple of days of rest before flying on to Lubbock.

Jo Ann was in a familiar bind: not wanting to turn her son away, on the one hand, and on the other, worried about what would happen if Jack returned from California early to find him back home. After John spent one night at home, she told him he would have to spend the next night—the night before he was to fly back to Lubbock—at a motel in case Jack came home.

John was crushed. Rejection: first Jodie, now his mother. "How am I going to get to the airport tomorrow?" he whined. Jo Ann hesitated, then softened, agreeing to return in the morning to take him.[18] When she did, the hurt still remained in his eyes.

It was not only hurt; beneath it there was anger—probably a decade's accumulation of anger. John Hinckley had decided that he was going to get even. But how? He couldn't bring himself to strike out at his parents directly, certainly not at his mother, and he couldn't hurt his father without hurting her. But he could embarrass them. He could make them regret the way they had treated him all these years. Guilt, that was it. He could make them feel responsible for some terrible thing he did. He had contemplated suicide for months, probably years, the thoughts expressed in the morbid, self-deprecating poems he had written. Instead he chose assassination—after considering mass murder—like many of the people he had read about after his exile to Lubbock.[19] It was an extraordinary act that no one, especially Jodie Foster and his parents, could ignore.

Despair, Perversity, and Political Targets

When John Hinckley left New Haven the third week of September, he didn't fly directly home. Instead he took a train to Washington. When she found out, Jo Ann assumed that he had spent a couple of days "sightseeing." Actually Hinckley's trip to Washington marked the beginning of his presidential stalk. After his brief, melancholy sojourn in Evergreen with his mother, he flew to Lubbock, where he purchased two more .22 caliber handguns at Snidely Whiplash's gun shop,[20] bringing his total to three. He also bought three thousand dollars worth of traveler's checks. By this time Hinckley was tracking President Jimmy Carter's movements through articles he read, and often clipped, in the *New York Times*. On September 27 he again flew to Washington. The next day he flew to Columbus, Ohio, to await Carter's visit. Two days later he took a bus to Dayton. On October 2 Hinckley was in Dayton, standing in a crowd of well-wishers when Carter arrived. Carter, smiling and waving, walked into the crowd to within a handshake of Hinckley. Claiming later that he was unarmed, Hinckley said he just wanted to see if he could get close enough to shoot.[21]

On October 6 Hinckley flew to Lincoln, Nebraska, in a futile attempt to interview a member of the American Nazi party. On October 7 he flew to Nashville to prepare for Carter's visit there later in the week. On October 9, the day Carter was to arrive, he was arrested at the Nashville airport with three handguns in his suitcase. The guns were confiscated, and he was fined and released after being held four or five hours. Shaken, Hinckley then destroyed a diary that he had been keeping—in the manner of Arthur Bremer, whose published diary Hinckley had read—for fear that it would have been too incriminating had the authorities bothered to examine it after his arrest. Undoubtedly the diary contained references to his designs on Carter, much as Bremer's had on Nixon and Wallace.[22]

After his release the police dropped Hinckley off at the airport and he flew to New Haven. Then he phoned his sister in Dallas to ask if it would be convenient for him to stop by for a visit with his little nephew. Later the same day, October 11, he flew to Dallas. While in Dallas he went to Rocky's Police Equipment and purchased two .22 caliber pistols to replace two of the three guns the police had confiscated. On October 15 he flew back to New Haven; two days later he was in Washington; and two days after that he was back in Evergreen.[23] When he left Dallas, his sister wasn't sure whether he was going back to New Haven for "another seminar" or to Los Angeles, unaware that her brother had Jimmy Carter on his mind.[24]

Hinckley's choice of Carter had nothing to do with the president's personality, or Carter's politics; nor did it have anything to do with Hinckley's father's politics. Jack

Hinckley was a staunch conservative, critical of Carter, and a strong supporter of the Republican nominee, Ronald Reagan. Hinckley decided to kill Carter simply because he was the president, someone whose prominence—whatever his policies—would ensure notoriety for the person who killed him. Hinckley, like Bremer, understood that if he had the guts to do it, his name would be on the lips of every anchorman on the network news, and it would be spelled out in the headlines of the nation's newspapers. No matter where Jack Hinckley was, zealously trying to save the world, Carter's assassination would be something he couldn't miss.

But John Hinckley did miss Carter—or, more accurately, he stopped trying. By the middle of October all the polls were predicting that Carter would be defeated. Most suggested that it wouldn't even be close. Hinckley wasn't going to make the same mistake as Arthur Bremer. Bremer, he believed, had moved down "a few pegs" when, failing to get President Nixon, he shot candidate George Wallace instead.[25] He would wait for the *new* president. It wouldn't be a long wait. By the third week of October John was back in Evergreen, sitting in the stony silence of the living room. Jack, as usual, was in his huge brown easy chair, staring angrily at the burning logs in the fireplace. His son sat across the room, head down like a disobedient puppy. The unspoken knowledge of the abortive writer's workshop, and the squandered $3,600 that went into it, filled the room like unwanted company. Jo Ann, as usual, sat between them. Yet another frustrating discussion about John's future eventually broke the silence before John left the room complaining of a headache. Jack, shaking his head, got up and walked to his study.[26]

Later that evening, as the Hinckleys prepared for bed, Jo Ann suggested that they seek professional help for John. They had tried everything else. Jack agreed. The next morning he called Darrell Benjamin, a psychologist who consulted with Vanderbilt Energy, and asked him to recommend a psychiatrist.[27] Benjamin recommended Dr. John Hopper. Hopper had an office right there in Evergreen, eliminating the need for Jo Ann to drive her son into Denver. An appointment was made for the following week, October 28. Two days before the appointment John took a Valium overdose. "I think I might have taken too many," he volunteered sheepishly to his mother. He went on to say that he had been "throwing up all day." But he had waited until Jack was gone before he told her.[28]

The overdose—and the fact that Hinckley reported it to his mother—can be considered what is sometimes called a suicidal "gesture," an attention-getting mechanism for some, an early warning signal for others. Jo Ann Hinckley was too upset about her son to have confidence in such subtle distinctions when she took John to see Dr. Hopper for the first time. She was relieved that the first session seemed to go well. Two more appointments for John were scheduled for the following week, and joint sessions were agreed upon where she, Jack, and John would meet together with Dr. Hopper. John's attitude seemed to improve somewhat.[29] He was once more the object of everyone's attention.

Being that object was also John's way of passively expressing anger toward his father. He never argued very long or talked back. That would have been easier for Jack to deal with. John understood that it was his passivity—his moody silences and inactivity, the poor-little-me look on his face—that really got under Jack's skin.

As did the overdose. Jack couldn't take any more of his son's stunts. A few days after the overdose incident he left for Africa to work on a World Vision project, more worried now about how to salvage his badly listing marriage than about a son he could no longer bear to be around. He admitted later that he "couldn't honestly have said which was the stronger drive, to help people in drought-stricken Africa, or to get away from Evergreen."[30]

John, of course, was glad his father was gone. Things were always easier, more relaxed, when Jack wasn't around. When they both were home, John never left his room in the mornings until he heard his father drive off to work. Then he would emerge to eat the breakfast his mother would prepare for him. After breakfast he would often sit in the living room, lounging in Jack's big easy chair—the "throne," as John called it. When he heard the sound of Jack's car in the driveway, he would scurry downstairs to the seclusion of his first-floor bedroom. On those occasions when Jo Ann suggested that he remain, for a change, to visit with his father, John would grumble, "Dad doesn't want to talk to me. He doesn't even want me in the house."[31] There was little Jo Ann could say to deny that.

On November 30, the day before Jack returned from Africa, John left for Washington. He spent a good part of December stalking President-elect Reagan. The stalk was interrupted on December 8 when Beatles star, John Lennon, was murdered by Mark David Chapman outside his apartment house in New York. Hinckley was very distressed and left for New York immediately. He spent much of the next week standing vigil outside Lennon's apartment building with other mourners. He also had a sexual encounter—like Arthur Bremer's, his first—with a teenage prostitute.[32] Later that month when he returned home for the Christmas holidays, his first words to his father were, "Don't make any cracks about Lennon, Dad. I'm in deep mourning."[33] It was one of the very few occasions on which he had ever spoken aggressively to his father.

Throughout this period Hinckley continued to make trips, wandering between Evergreen, Washington, New York, and New Haven, where he continued to make futile attempts to see Jodie Foster. In February he began to consider other possible targets for the frustration and anger gnawing at his insides. His reading had given Hinckley an informed grasp of the history of American violence. That month, following the lead of Oswald and Sirhan in his choice of victims, he waited in the corridor outside Senator Edward Kennedy's office on one occasion; on another he got as far as a metal detector leading into the U.S. Senate chamber before giving up the idea of a mass murder there, imitating the attack made by Puerto Rican nationalists in 1954. He browsed among the tourists on a White House tour with assassination on his mind. And on every disappointing trip to New Haven he continued to weigh the possibilities of a mass murder on the Yale campus in an attack much like the one made by Charles Whitman at the University of Texas in 1966 and the one Arthur Bremer considered in Milwaukee in 1972.[34]

Throughout this period he continued to see Dr. Hopper when he was in Evergreen. But he was gone much of the time, traveling the circuit between New Haven and Washington with a stop along the way in New York, where he continued to seek out underage prostitutes. No one—neither Dr. Hopper nor Hinckley's parents—was curious enough to inquire about where he was going and what he was doing on these mysterious jaunts. They all knew that he made frequent trips to Washington, but no one ever inquired why. Dr. Hopper suggested that Hinckley's restless wanderings might be the first stirrings of an emerging independence that his parents wanted so desperately for him to develop.[35] For their part Jack and Jo Ann had seemingly reached such a state of crisis in their own marriage that, as a coping mechanism, they had adopted an out-of-sight, out-of-mind philosophy about their son's absences. With increasing regularity, when John returned to Evergreen, they left for someplace else. In his many sessions with Dr. Hopper Hinckley never revealed the violent crimes he was considering as his frustrations in New Haven and Evergreen continued to build, nor did he mention the extensive collection of articles on assassins and assassinations that he was accumulating in his room. Hinckley did mention his attraction to Jodie Foster and his depression about John Lennon's death, but Dr. Hopper never pursued either issue. Dr. Hopper was completely unaware, for example, that on January 21, 1981—in the midst of his therapy—John Hinckley had bought a Charter Arms .38 at Kawasaki West in Lakewood, Colorado.[36] It was just like the weapon Mark Chapman used to kill John Lennon six weeks before.

Dr. Hopper focused on the obvious problem, the one Jack had defined for him during their sessions together, John Hinckley's immaturity and his need to take responsibility for himself instead of continuing to rely on his mother.[37] What he failed to recognize and explore was Hinckley's chronic and deepening depression, his complete social isolation, and his growing inability to cope with his frustration and hostility. Dr. Hopper observed the blunted affect commonly associated with acute depression but didn't think it was important.[38] In similar fashion he didn't make much of the social isolation of his patient— even when he read in the autobiography he had asked Hinckley to write, "Because I have remained so inactive and reclusive over the past five years I have managed to remove myself from the real world."[39] And Dr. Hopper interpreted the hostility as being primarily a reflection of sibling jealousy and rivalry. Hinckley, he could tell, resented his older brother and sister.[40] But, most important, it was what John Hinckley was *doing*—not saying—that Dr. Hopper missed in his diagnosis. There was nothing that John Hinckley *said* in all his sessions with Dr. Hopper that enabled the psychiatrist to recognize that he was dealing with a very dangerous patient.

Perhaps that was why Dr. Hopper's prescribed treatment matched his questionable diagnosis. The treatment amounted to more isolation, cushioned with what was, at that time, one of psychiatry's trendier cures—biofeedback therapy. It seemed to help some patients, and Dr. Hopper prescribed it for most. The therapy was to accompany a behaviorally oriented program of self-discipline defined by a formal contractual agreement between John and his parents. Accordingly, John had to assume certain responsibilities by mutually agreed upon deadlines: by the end of February he was to have a full-time job; by March 30 he was to have his own place to live. To John only the Marine Corps could have been worse. It was as if Jack had written the prescription himself.

On February 25 the Hinckleys flew to Phoenix for a stock holders' meeting followed by a few days at a guest ranch in Wickenburg, Arizona. When they returned on March 1, they found a note from John saying, "Your prodigal son has taken off again to exorcise some demons." As usual there was no hint as to where he had gone. Five days later the phone rang at 4:30 A.M. It was their son calling from New York with a familiar story: he was sick, hungry, and broke, and, of course, he wanted to come home. After much anguish over whether to send money—against Dr. Hopper's advice—Jack bought an airline ticket home, which John was to pick up at the Newark airport. The next day John called again to say that he didn't have enough money for busfare to the airport.

It is little wonder that Jack Hinckley was disgusted on March 7, when John got off the plane in Denver. Jack had to get it off his chest as he ushered his musty-smelling, unshaven son to a vacant boarding area. "You've broken every promise you've made to your mother and me," he began. "Our part of the agreement [arranged by Dr. Hopper] was to provide you a home and an allowance while you worked at becoming independent. I don't know what you've been doing these past months, but it hasn't been that, and we've reached the end of our rope." Jack handed him two hundred dollars and suggested that he move into the YMCA. "From here on you're on your own," he said. "Do whatever you want to." Jack later recalled that John had "looked at me like he couldn't believe his ears."[41]

In John Hinckley's unstated view his father had also broken the agreement. The agreement was that he had twenty-three more days before moving out. In Hinckley's mind it was another heartless, forced departure. The next time Jack Hinckley spoke to his son was on March 30, 1981. It was a phone call at 8:30 P.M. from a jail in Washington.[42] After that Jack Hinckley couldn't get that look in his son's eyes out of his mind.[43]

Chapter Three

ON BEING MAD OR
MERELY ANGRY

JACK HINCKLEY wasted no time or money in arranging for attorneys for his son's defense. He got some of the best: a team led by Vincent Fuller, a partner in the prestigious Williams and Connelly firm in Washington. This was not going to be the legal vaudeville act that Arthur Bremer's trial had been nine years before, twenty-five miles away in the rustic county courthouse in tiny Upper Marlboro, Maryland.

Hinckley's attorneys made two unsuccessful efforts to strike a plea agreement to avoid trial. They proposed that their client was willing to plead guilty to all counts against him in exchange for a Justice Department recommendation that he be permitted to serve the sentences he received on each count concurrently instead of consecutively. Consecutive sentences would amount to life in prison; concurrent sentences would mean that Hinckley would be eligible for parole in fifteen years. Government attorneys were in no mood to bargain in a case of this magnitude. When they rejected the offer the second time, Hinckley's attorneys entered a plea of Not Guilty By Reason of Insanity.[1]

Months later, when the jury announced its verdict acquitting Hinckley on all counts, prosecuting attorneys Roger Adelman, Robert Chapman, Marc Tucker, and Constance Belfiore were astonished. So were the psychiatrists who testified for them. Outrage spilled across editorial pages around the nation. It was a controversial verdict based on often confusing and contradictory psychiatric testimony.

THE INSANITY DEFENSE

Was John Warnock Hinckley, Jr., really mad on March 30, 1981, when he wrote that letter to Jodie Foster, describing what he was about to do? Was he criminally insane, as a jury finally decided, a person who could not be held accountable for the pain that he had brought to so many people? Or was he actually just an angry young man, emotionally disturbed, unquestionably, but one who was fully aware of what he was doing and who simply didn't care?

The evidence that John Hinckley had psychological difficulties was overwhelming, and testimony about it consumes thousands of pages of the trial transcripts: the childhood fears that probably gave rise to his timidity; the consequent social withdrawal that accelerated during his adolescence and led to the almost total isolation of his adult years; the abnormal dependence on his indulgent mother; the ulcerated relationship with his demanding father; the hypochondria and other attention-seeking behavior; the wandering existence; the morbid poetry; the interest in violent people; and the fantasies about an unattainable woman. It was not the psychological evidence itself that psychiatrists on either side of the case disagreed about but its interpretation—in particular, the incidents and behavior described in Chapter Two.

The two key prosecution witnesses, psychiatrists Sally Johnson and Park Dietz, didn't question the defense team's claim that John Hinckley was a troubled young man. They both agreed that he had a "narcissistic personality disorder." His social isolation alone (not a single friend could be identified) suggested a serious disturbance. But both maintained that, as Dietz put it, "his state of mind was influenced very little, if at all, by the disorders I have diagnosed."[2] In other words, both Johnson and Dietz believed that Hinckley was in control of himself at all times and was fully aware of what he was doing.

The test of insanity in the legal statutes of the District of Columbia hinges on the American Law Institute's Model Penal Code and the so-called Brawner rule, which defines mental illness as "any abnormal condition of the mind, regardless of its medical label, which substantially affects mental or emotional processes and substantially impairs [the defendant's] behavior controls. . . ." A defendant cannot be held responsible if, because of his mental illness, he "lacks substantial capacity either to appreciate the wrongfulness of his conduct or to conform his conduct to the requirements of the law."[a] To put it differently, the jury is required to answer two questions: Did the defendant have a mental disease or defect? If so, was that disease or defect the reason for the unlawful act? Johnson's and Dietz's answers to these questions were: yes, Hinckley was mentally disturbed, but no, that disturbance did not "cause" him to shoot the president. The three psychiatrists and one psychologist who testified for the defense answered yes to both questions, maintaining that Hinckley was living in a world of "delusions," which caused his actions.[3]

The most difficult task was borne by the prosecuting attorneys. It was they who had to prove "beyond a reasonable doubt" that John Hinckley's acknowledged mental "defects" had nothing to do with his shooting of the president and three other persons. If a reasonable doubt remained after the evidence was weighed, the jury was instructed to find Hinckley Not Guilty by Reason of Insanity.

Unlike the simpler M'Naghten rule, the Brawner rule set a standard that clearly favored the defense. Whereas the M'Naghten rule also required answers to two questions, they were usually much easier to answer than those posed by the Brawner standard: Did the defendant know what he

---

[a] The Model Penal Code 4.01 (P.O.D. 1962) is a refinement of the earlier (1954) Durham rule that broadened the definition of "mental disease" to include emotional as well as cognitive disabilities. See Durham v. United States, 214 F.2d 862 (U.S. Court of Appeals, D.C., 1954); and MacDonald v. United States, 312 F.2d 847, 851 (D.C. Cir. 1962).

was doing when he committed the crime? Did he understand that his actions were wrong? In the eyes of most
prosecutors the M'Naghten standard was not so easily clut-
tered up with the ambiguous, often nonempirical, language of psychiatry. Mental illness didn't matter as long as
the defendant was aware of the moral consequences of his
actions. If he was aware, then he could be held accountable
for his actions; if he wasn't, then he couldn't.[b]

Both teams of psychiatrists shared and drew their conclusions from the same body of evidence; which covered a
wide range of factors about John Hinckley's personality
and life. The defense, for example, insisted that his attempt
to have his songs published in Hollywood was evidence of
his grandiose delusions; Park Dietz, for the prosecution,
argued that the trip was simply the stuff of "hopes and
dreams" that most people have and that are perfectly normal.[4] Similarly, Hinckley's imaginary California girlfriend
Lynn was seen by the defense as further evidence of his
delusional mind. Not so, countered Sally Johnson: Lynn
was someone Hinckley consciously invented to manipulate
his parents or, as he explained to Johnson, "to get them off
my back." Every mention of Lynn, the prosecution pointed
out, was accompanied by a request for money.[5] In John
Hinckley's mind Lynn Collins was no more real than the
writer's workshop he invented for the same purpose—to
pry money out of his parents.

The attempts to woo actress Jodie Foster were described
as "bizarre" by defense psychiatrist, David Bear, "a sign of
disordered thought." The would-be tryst was not the result
of bizarre and disordered thought, the prosecution maintained; it was simply based on "poor judgment," a very
common frailty, and hardly associated with mental disease.[6] On the contrary, Park Dietz testified, Hinckley had a
very realistic grasp of his chances with Jodie Foster and

[b] In 1982 only sixteen states still used the less flexible "right-wrong"
cognitive standard of M'Naghten. Most, like the District of Columbia, had
adopted some variation of the Model Penal Code.

suggested as much when he wrote to her, "Even a phone conversation seems to be asking too much, but really I can't blame you for ignoring a little twerp like me." He never lost sight of the fact that when it came down to the issue of whether Jodie Foster would eventually succumb to his advances, the odds were very much against him.[7]

The defense made much of Hinckley's attempts to imitate the Travis Bickle character, insisting that Hinckley came to believe that he *was* Bickle. Nonsense, Dietz argued in lengthy testimony: while Hinckley "imitated" Bickle— dressing like him, buying guns, stalking a political candidate, consorting with teenage prostitutes in New York, even drinking peach brandy (as Bickle did) once in front of his parents—he never lost sight of the fact that he *was* John Hinckley.[8] It was hard to believe that a person who described himself as "Mr. Insignificant" and "a little twerp" actually thought he was the tough, swaggering Travis Bickle. Even Dr. Thomas C. Goldman, testifying for the defense, had to admit during cross-examination that John Hinckley was never confused about who he was.[9] In fact, it could be argued that John Hinckley knew precisely who he was; the problem was that that image of himself was something he couldn't accept and was trying desperately to change.

Since so much has been made of the impact *Taxi Driver* had on Hinckley's mind, it is worth mentioning a point that neither the prosecution nor the defense addressed: while Hinckley was attracted to the character Jodie Foster played in the film, Iris, he did not fall in love with Iris. There was never any confusion between the character and the actress; it was always the real Jodie Foster he pursued, not the fictitious Iris. In contrast, Hinckley was impressed with the fictitious Travis Bickle and not the real actor, Robert DeNiro, who played that part. On the stopovers in New York he made on the many trips between Evergreen, New Haven, and Washington, Hinckley never once tried to contact or see DeNiro, who spends much of his time there. Was this because by then he believed he was Bickle and DeNiro, therefore, did not exist? Or was it because he recognized that DeNiro and Bickle were two entirely different people—one real, the other imagined—just as Jodie Foster and Iris were? Hinckley was well aware that Robert DeNiro, like Jodie Foster, did not live and behave like the characters he played on the screen. There is little to suggest that Hinckley was ever so unsettled about his own identity that he thought he was someone else. John Hinckley never lost his ability to distinguish between the real world and characters he saw portrayed on the screen. When he wanted to see Jodie Foster, he went to New Haven; when he wanted sex with a teenage prostitute like Iris, he went to New York.

THE MALINGERING ISSUE

Complicating these issues was the accusation made by the prosecution that Hinckley had been able to manipulate the psychiatrists who were called to testify in his behalf, just as he had so often manipulated his parents. Hinckley, like his predecessor Arthur Bremer, was familiar with the art of malingering, or faking mental illness. He had read two books, at least, that discuss the issue in some detail. One was Robert Kaiser's book on the Sirhan Sirhan trial, *R.F.K. Must Die!*, which delves into the psychological shenanigans that characterized the trial; the other was Eliot Asinof's *The Fox Is Crazy Too*, a true story of the skyjacker Garrett Trapnell, which explains how Trapnell skillfully faked symptoms of paranoia in an attempt to escape punishment.

There were also hints that maybe the problem went beyond simple manipulation on Hinckley's part, that defense psychiatrists were cooperating in the effort and had actually coached Hinckley during their interviews with him to make it appear that he was more disturbed than he actually was. Park Dietz charged that such coaching had become part of the defense's "legal strategy."[10] These were serious charges, calling into question the competence and ethics of expert witnesses for the defense; at least one of the government attorneys was also concerned that ethical lapses had occurred.

At issue was Hinckley's interest in John Lennon's killer, Mark David Chapman. The prosecution claimed that Hinckley discovered the "parallel" between himself and Chapman after reading an article his attorneys gave him, comparing them. Dr. Sally Johnson, who had spent the longest time with Hinckley, interviewing him almost daily for a period of four months while Hinckley was confined at the Federal Correctional Institute in Butner, North Carolina, testified that Hinckley had told her that his attorneys had consulted with Chapman's attorneys on the issue.[11] Still, it was hard to dismiss the fact that Hinckley had purchased a Charter Arms revolver like Chapman's right after Lennon's murder, long before Hinckley's psychiatrists got hold of him. That didn't appear to be merely a coincidence.

But Johnson also testified, more convincingly, that Hinckley's fund of information about the symptoms of schizophrenia, and the influence *Taxi Driver* could have had on his actions, increased dramatically after he began to meet with his own psychiatrists. Not only was he supplied with articles in a psychological vein that had been written about him, Hinckley had even been permitted to review the symptoms of schizophrenia explained in the *Diagnostic and Statistical Manual III* of the American Psychiatric Association.[12] One of his psychiatrists, Dr. William Carpenter, admitted under questioning that he had gone over the material with Hinckley, page by page, asking him whether he had any of the symptoms listed. Dr. Carpenter came under attack again when the prosecution charged that he had suggested to Hinckley various interpretations of poems the defendant had written, all of which were slanted toward Carpenter's diagnosis of schizophrenia. Carpenter admitted questioning Hinckley about the "meaning" of the poetry but denied that it was his intention to *suggest* meaning to him.[13]

The charges didn't stop there. Dr. Johnson also testified that after a session with Dr. Thomas C. Goldman, Hinckley told her that he was "no longer sure" whether Lynn, the girlfriend he had fabricated, was real or not. Up until that time, she said, he had laughed about the way he had invented Lynn to deceive his parents.[14]

Perhaps the most startling revelation was that Hinckley had been given the report one of his psychiatrists, Dr. David Bear, had written about him. When questioned about the incident, Bear claimed that he was surprised when he received a letter from Hinckley, critiquing the report and making corrections and suggestions where he saw fit. In particular, Hinckley wanted Dr. Bear to mention his "White House fantasy," a story Hinckley claimed he had somehow failed to relate during their sessions together. Hinckley wanted Dr. Bear to make an insertion in the report to document a bizarre claim that he tried to assassinate the president so that he and Jodie Foster could move into the White House.[15]

The circumstances, substance, and timing of Hinckley's suggestions were suspicious. The prosecution claimed it was purely manipulation: an attempt, by Hinckley, to get Dr. Bear to include in his report new material that was designed to bolster his insanity defense by bringing Dr. Bear's conclusions in line with the diagnoses of schizophrenia that Hinckley knew Dr. Carpenter and Dr. Goldman had already submitted.[16]

Since most of the accusations were based on information Hinckley himself had given to Dr. Sally Johnson over the lengthy period he had spent with her, the irregularities in the way Hinckley's psychiatrists had handled his case were undeniable and difficult to explain. Dr. Johnson had obviously become someone Hinckley felt he could confide in, probably more so than anyone in his entire life, including his mother. Hinckley's attorney, Vincent Fuller, tried to discount these revelations and Hinckley's candor with Johnson by suggesting that his client was attracted to her and was just trying to impress her by telling her what he thought she wanted to hear.[17]

Possibly. But Fuller's argument was weakened when he then argued that Hinckley was less than candid—and therefore did not reveal the true seriousness of his illness—because he was ashamed to admit his problems when he was first evaluated by a three-member team of male doctors composed of Dietz and psychiatrists James Cavanaugh and Jonas Rappeport.[18] The 628-page report they prepared with the assistance of psychologist John Monahan on the basis of those interviews concluded that Hinckley, despite obvious problems, was criminally responsible.[c]

It was all very confusing, especially to the jury. Four psychiatrists and a psychologist were claiming that Hinckley was insane; three psychiatrists and a psychologist were claiming that he was not, suggesting that the only reason he might appear to be was largely because he had been shown how by his doctors. As the trial began to wind down, it seemed that John Hinckley was not the only one whose grasp of reality was in question.

Then the issue of the admissability of CAT-scan (computerized axial tomography) evidence was raised. The CAT-scan evidence consisted of three-dimensional X-rays of Hinckley's brain.[19] The X-rays were something tangible, something a jury could see, but the problem was one of interpretation. Medical experts were not sure how, if at all, such evidence was related to schizophrenia. There were no doubts, however, in Dr. Bear's mind. He was convinced that the Cat-scan evidence was essential to his diagnosis and risked a contempt citation by threatening to refuse to testify unless it was admitted.[20] After much legal hassling over the appropriateness and scientific validity of CAT-scan results as a means of diagnosing mental illness, a slide projector was brought into the courtroom with a new battery of experts to interpret what they saw. The X-rays showed that Hinckley's sulci—the spaces between the

---

[c] The report remains under seal at this writing.

skull and the brain—were wider than normal. But what did that mean?[21] Dr. Bear insisted that it suggested the probability of schizophrenia. Fewer than one in fifty normal people has such a condition, he testified, while it is present in one of three schizophrenics in treatment at nearby St. Elizabeths Hospital.[22] So what? said Roger Adelman during his cross-examination of Bear, pointing out that the statistic also meant that two-thirds of those schizophrenics had normal sulci. The relationship Bear described between the CAT-scan evidence and Hinckley's alleged schizophrenia, Adelman said, was illusory. Moreover, Adelman continued, there was as yet no scientific basis for assuming a causal link between such abnormalities and a patient's behavior.[23]

The controversy continued as more experts were brought in to interpret what the "widened sulci" around Hinckley's brain might imply about his behavior when he shot the president. After all the testimony it was apparent that the experts could not be sure.[24] Once again the significance of the evidence hinged on a subjective judgment that reflected the side of the case one happened to represent or sympathize with.

Jack Hinckley, with his engineer's perspective, expected more precision from these doctors, something more scientific for the thousands of dollars he was paying them. He wanted them to prove, in language everyone could understand, what he wanted to believe—that his son was not responsible for what he had done. Instead he got confusion, and it made him angry about "being treated to the spectacle of experts in the field voicing contradictory opinions, depending on which side had hired them, all the while claiming to be making unbiased scientific diagnoses . . . on every point, confusing not only the jury . . . but everyone else."[25]

The trial ended with a showing of *Taxi Driver*. The blood-drenched final scenes were disturbing. The zoom-in showing the dazed Bickle, sitting in the midst of the carnage, slowly raising his finger to his temple and squeezing an imaginary trigger, probably reminded the jury of the photograph John Hinckley had taken of himself in that pose with a real gun in his hand. The effect it had on the jury was impossible to gauge.

But after all the evidence was presented, it appeared to both sides that the best evidence of Hinckley's state of mind when he opened fire on March 30, 1981, was what they had started with: the letter he had written to Jodie Foster less than two hours before. Did he understand what he was about to do, and to whom? Did he understand the consequences for himself and others? In other words, was the shooting a deliberate act, or was it the result of something within himself that he could not understand or control?

Dear Jodie,

There is a definite possibility that I will be killed in my attempt to get Reagan. It is for this very reason that I am writing you this letter now.

As you well know by now I love you very much. Over the past seven months I've left you dozens of poems, letters and love messages in the faint hope that you could develop an interest in me. Although we talked on the phone a couple of times I never had the nerve to simply approach you and introduce myself. Besides my shyness, I honestly did not wish to bother you with my constant presence. I know the many messages left at your door and in your mailbox were a nuisance, but I felt that it was the most painless way for me to express my love for you.

I feel very good about the fact that you at least know my name and know how I feel about you. And by hanging around your dormitory, I've come to realize that I'm the topic of more than a little conversation, however full of ridicule it may be. At least you know that I'll always love you.

Jodie, I would abandon this idea of getting Reagan in a second if I could only win your heart and live out the rest of my life with you, whether it be in total obscurity or whatever.

I will admit to you that the reason I'm going ahead with this attempt now is because I just cannot wait any longer to impress you. I've got to do something now to make you understand, in no uncertain terms, that I am doing all of this for your sake! By sacrificing my freedom and possibly my life, I hope to change your mind about me. This letter is being written only an hour before I leave for the Hilton Hotel. Jodie, I'm asking you to please look into your heart and at least give me the chance, with this historical deed, to gain your respect and love.

He closed with "I love you forever," and it was signed like all his previous notes to her, "John Hinckley"—not Travis Bickle.[26]

In his closing argument for the prosecution Roger Adelman recounted what seemed to be overwhelming evidence that Hinckley's attack on the president was a cold-blooded, deliberate act. It doesn't matter what his reasons for shooting Reagan and three others were, Adelman insisted. What matters, he continued, is that the evidence makes it clear that John Hinckley was fully aware of his actions before, during, and after the shooting. Then he reminded the jury about the stalking, the letter to Jodie Foster, his deliberate selection of the six deadly "devastator" bullets from among the ordinary ammunition he had in his possession, the practiced posture he assumed during the shooting, and, after his arrest, the jokes with police officers and his inquiry to the FBI and Secret Service agents about whether television coverage of the shooting would preempt the Academy Award presentations that evening. All these *actions*, Adelman insisted, left little doubt about Hinckley's deadly intentions. He saw himself as an assassin, Adelman said. The phrase "this historical deed" in his letter to Jodie Foster was lifted from the diary of Lee Harvey Oswald![27]

When Vincent Fuller began his closing argument for the defense, Jack Hinckley was convinced that only a miracle could offset the damage of Adelman's savagely thorough summation of evidence against his son.[28] Compared to Adelman, Fuller seemed weary as he began to go over the psychiatric testimony and events in Hinckley's troubled life. But then he focused on the letter. "It was delusional thinking," he said, "pure and simple." Indisputable and "pathetic" evidence of a very sick mind. How, he asked the jury, could anyone think that he could "impress" a woman he loved by shooting the president, unless he was insane?[29]

John Hinckley began to weep. The last time Jack had seen his son cry was when he was in the first grade. That was also about the last time he had given his boy a hug.[30]

Maybe it was the letter, or maybe it was the CAT-scan evidence—the psychiatric testimony was just too contradictory to have had much impact—but the jury decided that there was a "reasonable doubt" about John Hinckley's sanity. Jack and Jo Ann Hinckley were jubilant as they embraced each other, their attorneys, and each of the jurors. When the courtroom emptied, marshals led them down to the basement cell where their son was waiting. The three embraced and then joined hands as Jack gave thanks. "Lord, we asked You for a miracle," he prayed. "I gave up believing in it long ago, but You granted it just the same. Thank You, dear Lord. Thank You."[31]

Later, looking back on his son's life, Jack said, "If I had any guilt about the kind of father I'd been for John, it was that I failed to praise him when he did something well. . . . I'd never understood the importance of a father's praise— probably because I'd never experienced it. Never once could I recall Kib Brooks complimenting me. To any achievement his response was invariably: 'That's O.K., Jack, but you can do better.' "[32]

But he said that he hadn't praised the two older children, Scott and Diane, either. Maybe so; perhaps they had not suffered the absence of praise because they were older when the family moved to Dallas, more insulated in school from the pressures at home, less dependent on their parents for a sense of self-esteem.

Still, it was hard to believe that Jack hadn't taken more pride in Scott and Diane, that he hadn't acknowledged them more than he had John. After all, his new company had been named Vanderbilt Energy because of his pride in

Scott's graduation from that fine old Southern institution. And everyone who knew the Hinckleys soon learned that Diane had been a head cheerleader, vice-president of the mixed choir, a Homecoming Queen nominee, and a member of the National Honor Society at Southern Methodist—they knew because Jack told them.

Expensive private schools were selected for Scott and Diane, but a prosaic state school on the dusty plains of West Texas was considered good enough for John. Moreover, the Hinckleys rarely said a word about their youngest son. Until the assassination attempt "I didn't even know John existed," said one Evergreen neighbor who had accompanied Jack and Jo Ann on a European trip. And that was true for most of their friends. John Hinckley had become a family embarrassment long before he shot the president.[33]

Chapter Four

CHANGING SIDES

NOT long after his arrival at St. Elizabeths Hospital John Hinckley underwent a major psychiatric evaluation. The results seemed to support his attorneys' arguments at the trial. John Hinckley, his doctors reported in their "Bolton Report," suffered from a "major depressive disorder" with "schizotypal," "schizoid," and "narcissistic" dimensions. Moreover, they concluded, "his defective reality testing and impaired judgement combined with his capacity for planned and impulsive behaviors makes him an unpredictably dangerous person. Mr. Hinckley is presently a danger to himself, Jodie Foster and to any other third party whom he would consider incidental in his ultimate aims."[1]

To anyone who read the report, it appeared that John Hinckley would remain hospitalized for a long, long time. Now that the trial was over, that was exactly what the government attorneys who prosecuted him wanted to believe. They didn't think that Hinckley's acknowledged psychological problems were sufficient to justify his insanity acquittal, but they heartily agreed with the St. Elizabeths doctors that John W. Hinckley, Jr., was a very dangerous young man.

But from that point forward Hinckley seemed to respond to the antidepressant and antipsychosis medication and the therapy he was given. Late in 1983 his depression began to lift, and his obsession with Jodie Foster, and the violent fantasies of rape and murder that accompanied it, began to subside, or so his doctors said. Only his attention-seeking behavior, symptomatic of his "narcissism," continued—for example, a bizarre letter he had written to a *New York Times* reporter[2] in 1982 after his acquittal and a troubling interview with *Penthouse* in the following year.

"What is a typical day like at St. Elizabeths?" *Penthouse* asked.

"I see a therapist, answer mail, play my guitar, listen to music, play pool, watch television, eat lousy food, and take delicious medication," Hinckley replied, noting that some patients "ask for my autograph."

Not much had changed about John Hinckley—or the way he lived—after his hospitalization. He was still the same self-absorbed person, except now he was famous and less isolated.

"Do you enjoy or resent the attention you are getting?"

"I'd be a liar if I said I resented it," Hinckley replied. "Because of my notoriety I do have certain restrictions placed on me here at St. Elizabeths, and I certainly don't like this aspect of my fame."[3]

It was that restrictive "aspect" of his "fame" that Hinckley decided to change after the interview when he requested telephone privileges. He also asked that the hospital stop censoring his mail. The hospital lifted both restrictions in 1984. It was part of his therapy, his doctors reasoned. Hinckley's pattern of complete social isolation had to be broken if he was to improve. Broadening his social contacts by phone and letters was one way to do it.

Hinckley was quick to take advantage of these new privileges, and his gradual improvement seemed to accelerate. The bizarre letters and interviews stopped. His doctors read this as a good sign. Hinckley seized the opening. A few months after the first privileges had been granted, he filed a formal complaint about the conditions of his confinement. He wanted additional privileges. A year later, in 1985, his privileges were expanded further to include "accompanied" strolls around the hospital grounds.[4]

On his own initiative in February 1986 he filed a Motion for Conditional Release.[5] It included two requests: a transfer to "a less restrictive ward" and "city privileges one day per month." For city privileges Hinckley had in mind being permitted to spend one day a month unaccompanied, in Washington, without any restrictions on his movements.[6]

An annoyed hospital staff unanimously recommended that the court deny both requests. Hinckley had overplayed his hand.

Joseph Henneberry, director of Forensic Programs at St. Elizabeths, put it this way in his affidavit: "It is not clinically appropriate that Mr. Hinckley be granted city privileges. It is not possible to state that Mr. Hinckley would not present a danger to the community if granted such privileges at this time."[7]

At the court hearing on Hinckley's requests, on March 24, 1986, his psychiatrist, Dr. Joan A. Turkus, testified that Hinckley's condition had improved during his hospitalization, but she noted that he was still taking Trilafon, a medication for psychosis, and Imipramine for his depression. She said his condition continued to warrant the ward restrictions he objected to. Foremost among her reasons for recommending denial of Hinckley's request for city privileges, she said, was "Mr. Hinckley's own history and the history of dangerous behavior that he has displayed in the past. And the other is his own clinical condition, in which he still has a major mental illness. . . . He is no longer psychotic and depressed," she testified, "but he does have a serious narcissistic personality disorder."[8] Hinckley still craved attention, his judgment was flawed, and he was impulsive and insensitive to others. But before the year had ended there was an important change in Dr. Turkus's assessment.

Just nine months after doctors denied his outrageous request for city privileges—the request itself, was viewed by some as further evidence of his narcissistic disorder—John Hinckley left the hospital with an escort and traveled to Reston, Virginia, tailed by the Secret Service. It was December 28, 1986, and the hospital had given Hinckley a twelve-hour pass for a holiday visit with his family at a center run by Prison Fellowship Ministries, an organization supported by his father. A week before the visit the hospital notified the Secret Service of their plans.[9] Both the Secret Service and government attorneys objected to the surprising decision but were powerless to do anything about it.

"This was a decision made by the hospital," a spokesman for the Secret Service said. "It was a *medical* decision they made over our objections. Our evaluation of Mr. Hinckley hasn't changed. We still feel him to be a threat to our protectees."[10]

There was obvious disagreement on whether John Hinckley remained a dangerous person. Government attorneys decided to look into the statutory basis of the hospital's controversial unilateral decision before Hinckley was released again. They thought it curious that the hospital's assessment of Hinckley had changed so completely in such a relatively short period of time.[11]

A few months later, on March 23, 1987, St. Elizabeths notified the court that it again recommended that Hinckley be permitted another visit with his family, off hospital grounds, over the Easter holidays—this time without a hospital escort.[12] Noting significant improvement in Hinckley's "impulse control" and "judgement" since a suicide attempt in 1983, the letter, signed by the hospital superintendent and two forensic specialists, went on to say that the hospital's assessment of Hinckley had been confirmed in an "independent opinion" by a psychiatric consultant, Dr. Glenn Miller.

Both Dr. Miller and Hinckley's own doctor, Joan A. Turkus, agreed, the letter explained, "that Mr. Hinckley has changed substantially since 1982, finding none of the earlier pathological thinking seen at the time of the Bolton evaluation present. Dr. Miller also noted," the letter continued, "that Mr. Hinckley is demonstrating an increased sense of responsibility for his unlawful acts and an appropriate guilt response. . . . It is the hospital's opinion that Mr. Hinckley does not pose a danger to himself or others if granted this limited privilege."[13]

The government attorneys who prosecuted Hinckley didn't agree. "We do not believe that anyone who tries to nullify a national election with a bullet deserves the privilege of moving freely in a civilized society," U.S. Attorney Joseph E. diGenova said as his assistants began a mad scramble to block the decision. On April 7, 1987, they submitted a motion to the court requiring the court's approval before Hinckley could be released from the hospital grounds.[14] The issue before the court was, on one side, the hospital's obligation to treat Hinckley's illness in a manner most beneficial to his recovery and, on the other, the court's obligation to protect the public from a violent offender who might still be dangerous. There seemed to be little question that Hinckley's behavior within the tightly regulated hospital environment had improved. At issue was Hinckley's potential dangerousness outside that controlled institutional setting. Was he no longer dangerous, as his doctors claimed, or did he still pose a serious threat to society, as the Secret Service and government attorneys believed? It is perhaps the most difficult question mental health professionals are asked to answer about human behavior.

Government attorneys put it bluntly in their pleadings: "As this Court is aware, Mr. Hinckley has a long history of psychiatric problems which was presented in great detail at the trial." Then, taking a swipe at the doctor who had treated Hinckley before he shot the president, the statement continued, "As is evident from that history, if psychiatry was capable of predicting Mr. Hinckley's future dangerousness, there would never have been the need for a trial in this case."[15]

What the hospital did with Hinckley in terms of therapy and increasing his privileges *within* the hospital was one thing, the government argued. That was the hospital's responsibility, not the court's. But once the court is petitioned to release Hinckley into the *community*, "it is the Court, not his doctors, which must be convinced by clear and convincing evidence that he is now ready for release." Government attorneys didn't believe such evidence existed, and until it did, the hospital, they insisted, was obligated to treat Hinckley as dangerous until the court decided otherwise.[16]

John Hinckley's conduct at St. Elizabeths had changed for the better. He was friendlier, more sociable, and he denied having the old obsessions with Jodie Foster and the array of violent criminals he read about and seemingly identified with before he shot the president.

"I thought at the time [1982] that Mr. Hinckley was dangerous to Jodie Foster, possibly to the president, or any third party who might get in his way," Dr. Miller told Judge Barrington Parker at the hearing on Hinckley's release request on April 13, 1987. But, the doctor claimed, much about Hinckley had changed in the last four years as he had responded to treatment.[17]

Jodie Foster, Miller stated flatly, "is no longer an issue in his life." His views about her had changed, Miller claimed. Hinckley now realized that his feelings about the young actress were "ridiculous," even delusional, Miller continued.[18] "He told me that for the last several years she has not been any real part of his sexual or psychic life," Miller told the court, adding that Hinckley had told him that the Jodie Foster "fantasies" were a thing of the past. In fact, Miller said, there was now another woman in Hinckley's life. Hinckley had fallen in love with, and hoped to marry, another patient at St. Elizabeths—a woman who had shotgunned her seven-year-old daughter to death and then had blown off her own arm in a suicide attempt a few years before.[19]

For the first time Miller observed remorse in his patient. Miller said that Hinckley, "in a somewhat pointed way," had told him "that he remembered Mr. [James] Brady in his prayers, that at night in his prayers he would often ask that God would help Mr. Brady." Miller was impressed with this positive change in Hinckley's "psychological sensitivity."[20]

U.S. Assistant Attorney Roger Adelman, who had directed the prosecution six years before at Hinckley's trial, was a little bored and very skeptical as he listened to Hinckley's attorney, Vincent Fuller, eliciting the positive appraisal from Miller. Hinckley was beginning to sound more and more like a choirboy. But what Miller said next brought Adelman upright in his chair.

Fuller was gently leading his witness through a litany of his client's improvements: yes, his judgment is "certainly improved"; no, he no longer has "fantasies" about Jodie Foster; no, he no longer sees himself as a celebrity because he shot the president; no, he no longer sees people as "shadowbox figures," and so forth. "In all that he has changed," Miller said, "but his judgment is not perfect, however. . . . He writes letters to some of his pen pals."[21]

"Are there any particular examples that come to your mind as evidence of that?" Fuller asked, knowing he was going to get an answer he didn't want to hear but feeling he had to ask the question before Adelman did.

"He has written recently a letter to—I think his name is Bundy," Miller replied, "a convicted mass murderer in Florida—expressing his sorrow, as I understand it, his feelings [about] the awful position that Bundy must be in."[22]

Miller answered in matter-of-fact tones, seemingly unaware that the revelation was rocking the courtroom like a mortar round. Fuller responded only with a funny, suddenly blank expression.

"Is this in your recent—" Judge Parker stammered into the awkward silence.

"No," Miller interrupted, "I learned of this *after* [preparing the report on Hinckley]. I learned of the Bundy business from Dr. Turkus," Miller continued, mentioning along the way that his patient had corresponded with "Squeaky" Fromme and that Hinckley had also "requested Mr. [Charles] Manson's address." Then as if to deflect the implications of remarks that he just at that moment seemed to be realizing, Miller added lamely, "But so far as I know, he has never written a letter to Mr. Manson."[23]

Miller's seemingly innocent revelations about his patient's odd preferences in "pen pals" was news to the government attorneys opposing Hinckley's release. For some reason St. Elizabeths Hospital had withheld the information. Neither of the doctors who examined Hinckley—Dr. Miller or Dr. Turkus—had revealed any information about Bundy, Fromme, or Manson in their discussions with the government attorneys prior to the hearing, as they were required to do.[24] As it turned out, Hinckley's attorney, Vincent Fuller, said that he learned about the letters only the day before when Dr. Turkus mentioned it to him.[25] Realizing the significance of the information, Fuller apparently felt obligated—in a manner Hinckley's doctors did not—to bring it out at the hearing.[26] Much of Hinckley's earlier insanity defense had hinged on what he read and wrote. Now it appeared that his doctors were withholding just such pertinent information to enhance Hinckley's chances for an Easter holiday with his family.

It seemed that once Hinckley was acquitted and hospitalized, the positions of the government and his own attorneys reversed from what they had been at his trial. Now it was Hinckley's attorneys and doctors who were claiming he was responsible for his actions and, therefore, could be safely released into the community for periodic therapeutic visits. The same kind of materials (Hinckley's writing) that they had used to argue successfully that he was insane, they now wanted to suppress in order to further their plans for his release.

In contrast, government attorneys—who had dismissed the psychological significance of Hinckley's morbid poetry and other writing during the trial—were now ready to argue that Hinckley's letters were "clinically relevant" to the question of his release. The fact that the sides had switched positions was ironic, perhaps, but not unusual for an insanity case involving a violent offender.

With the aftereffects of Miller's revelations about Hinckley's pen pals still rippling through the courtroom, Roger Adelman asked for a court order directing Hinckley and Dr. Turkus "to disgorge and present" all correspondence and other information pertinent to the proceeding.[27] After much discussion of Hinckley's rights under these circumstances Adelman requested a search of his room at St. Elizabeths. He also insisted that a representative of the court be there when they did it. It was obvious that government attorneys had some reservations about the ethics and professional integrity of the St. Elizabeths staff.

This wasn't the first time that Hinckley's mail had gotten him into trouble. In addition to his letters to newspapers the court was aware that early in his hospitalization he had written to a young woman, Penny Bailey, in Chicago. Bailey had first written to Hinckley, offering to help kill Jodie Foster for him. In Hinckley's reply to her he suggested that Bailey "take the bus to New Haven, Connecticut where Jodie is in school, and kill her yourself."[28] He also asked Bailey to send him a .38 Special in a package to be used in an escape.

During the same period he had also written one James R. Snyder, a convicted murderer known for escape attempts. In his letter to Snyder Hinckley said, in part: "So when do you think you'll be a free man again? Five years? Ten years? Never? Do you have anything up your sleeve in the way of unscheduled departures? No need to go into details; I'm just curious."[29]

In his report prepared before learning of the Bundy correspondence Dr. Miller had written that Hinckley "appears to be a far different person" than he was four years earlier when he wrote those letters to Bailey and Snyder.[30] He continued to stick to that line in his testimony.

In spite of his own revealing of the Bundy letters and Hinckley's request for Manson's address Miller tried to downplay their significance. "I do not believe he is dangerous to himself," Miller insisted, "and I do not believe he is a danger to Jodie Foster, and I do not believe that he is a danger to Mr. Brady or Mr. Reagan at this time."

"[Is he dangerous] to anyone?" Judge Parker asked.

"I do not know," Miller admitted, hesitating on the contradiction, then plowing right through it. "I do not believe he is dangerous to himself or others at the present time."[31]

Government attorneys were not persuaded by Miller's confidence or his logic. It seemed to Roger Adelman that Miller was torn between what he wanted to say—and, perhaps, was *expected* to say—and his own uncertainty about whether his patient was dangerous or not. There was also great concern about the policies and practices at St. Elizabeths. It appeared that the hospital had deliberately withheld important information on Hinckley, and Adelman and his colleagues suspected that there might still be more that they were unaware of.

"The Bundy letters became known to Dr. Turkus, I believe, on April 7, 1987," Roger Adelman complained, "but had never been revealed to this Court until Dr. Miller testified about them [nearly a week later, on April 13]."[32]

"Well, Mr. Adelman, do you see anything deliberate about the activity of the hospital? Or are you suggesting that?" Judge Parker asked.[33]

"We have great concern. I'm not prepared to assign a qualitative adjective to it," Adelman replied, "but we are really concerned, your Honor, about what has been forthcoming from the hospital—whether we are getting the whole story. The Bundy letters are my point of departure. For goodness' sake, your Honor, here we have a situation where Mr. Hinckley is communicating with a mass murderer! Dr. Turkus, we learn, finds out about it April 7, makes *no* entry in the hospital records until *after* it's brought up, and finally makes an entry on April 13!"[34]

Judge Parker was persuaded. On April 14 he signed an order requiring that a search of Hinckley's hospital room be carried out that day. Hinckley's attorneys tried unsuccessfully to impose restrictions, claiming that an unrestricted search would constitute an invasion of Hinckley's privacy. But the court denied their motion, agreeing only to exclude photographs and family correspondence. The court did agree to protect Hinckley's privacy by sealing all materials from public scrutiny.

In the course of his remarks Adelman went on to suggest that Hinckley's interest in Bundy might have been sparked by a two-part television movie about the serial killer, *Desperate Stranger*, which had been shown amidst much publicity the previous year, 1986.[35] Recalling the defense strategy at Hinckley's trial, Adelman employed a new variation, alluding to a "parallel" between Hinckley's earlier interest in the *Taxi Driver* killer, Travis Bickle, and his present interest in Bundy.[36]

Vincent Fuller tried to discount the importance of the Bundy correspondence. Often during Hinckley's trial five years before, Fuller seemed to others to be uncomfortable with his client, frequently avoiding interactions with him, leaving that to his assistants. Now he seemed both uncomfortable and unconvincing as he tried to explain away the significance of Hinckley's mail.

"Well, I think it's significant, your Honor, that Dr. Turkus, in reading the Bundy materials, characterized them as being innocuous and not suggestive. What bothers me," Fuller continued, "is that Mr. Adelman yesterday stood here before your Honor and suggested that the Bundy letters suggested Mr. Hinckley was fascinated with the Bundy movie in much the same fashion he was with *Taxi Driver*. That's baseless. And today on the front page of the *Washington Post*, that's the lead of the story. And I think it is unfortunate."[37]

At that moment, as Judge Parker listened to Adelman and Fuller argue about the significance of Hinckley's correspondence, officials at St. Elizabeths were in a sweat over yet another embarrassing discovery. The court-ordered search of Hinckley's room completed the night before uncovered more evidence to support Roger Adelman's skepticism about the competence and honesty of the staff at the hospital.

Later the same day, April 15, St. Elizabeths surprised everyone by abruptly withdrawing its request for Hinckley's Easter release. In its letter to the court the hospital explained vaguely that it was doing so "for administrative reasons and in order to further assess the clinical significance of writings and other materials belonging to Mr. Hinckley," adding defensively that the materials "were heretofore unexamined by the hospital staff."[38]

The unspecified "other materials" consisted of twenty photographs of Jodie Foster that Hinckley had hidden in his room. All had been collected during his confinement. Technically speaking the court order had not included photographs, and the hospital was not, therefore, obligated to inform the court of its shocking discovery. But sensitized by the present uproar over Hinckley's correspondence, and probably aware that news of the photographs had already been leaked to the press, the hospital decided that it had no choice; it made its discovery known to the court shortly after it had withdrawn its release request.[39] It seemed that not only Hinckley's fascination with violent criminals but also his obsession with Jodie Foster were continuing in full bloom, his doctors' denials notwithstanding.

The hidden photographs were the last straw for government attorneys. They requested a full review of the policies and procedures of the Forensic Division at St. Elizabeths Hospital.

Earlier on the same day, April 16, that the hospital had notified the court about the Jodie Foster photographs Jack Hinckley appeared on NBC's *Today Show*. Unaware of the damaging new evidence found in his son's room, he was indignant. "We've been hearing all week that John is still dangerous and all sorts of other terrible things," Jack told his interviewer, "and a certain hysteria has developed that we feel is not necessary, not pertinent to the case. [John] wrote [Bundy] as one human being to another," the elder Hinckley insisted. "It may not be something that you or I would do, but because John did write him does not mean that he is still dangerous."[40] The next day *NBC Nightly News* broke the story about his son's collection of photographs.

Four days after Jack Hinckley's television appearance newspapers reported that Dr. Glenn Miller—who had testified so insistently in the face of contradictory information that Hinckley's behavior had improved under treatment—had been paid by Jack Hinckley for his assessment. "We were informed by St. Elizabeths that Dr. Miller had been compensated [by the Hinckleys] in response to a direct question," a spokesman for U.S. Attorney Joseph E. diGenova told reporters. A spokesman for the Hinckleys immediately denied the story. St. Elizabeths responded by denying that it had paid Miller.[41]

Who paid Dr. Miller? Or was it, as government attorneys suspected, that he had not *yet* been paid, making the denials on both sides easier? In the wake of controversy following his nonchalant mention of Hinckley's "pen pals," stirred anew by the discovery of the Jodie Foster photographs, it now seemed that no one wanted to claim Dr. Glenn Miller.

Earlier, at their son's trial, both Jack and Jo Ann Hinckley believed John's fascination with a sociopathic killer and an underage prostitute in *Taxi Driver* was another shocking and bizarre symptom of his disordered mind. Like the attorneys on either side of the issue, they had changed their perspective, backed as before by Jack's familiar determination and conviction—a determination and conviction that could have easily had its effect on the judgments of his son's doctors during the family therapy sessions he attended.

Jack Hinckley was a presence—and a force—that could not be easily dismissed. And he was accustomed to having his own way. Discounting the disturbing revelation about his son's continuing obsessions with the likes of Ted Bundy and Charles Manson, Jack had vowed on national television that they would try again to have John released "as soon as they [the hospital] think the hysteria has subsided and it's an appropriate time to do it."[42] He seemed to be suggesting that the problem was now public "hysteria," not his son's unyielding pattern of behavior.

The following October, six months after the hospital withdrew its request for Hinckley's Easter release, the National Institutes of Mental Health's Ad Hoc Forensic Advisory Panel released the report government attorneys had requested after the fiasco in April. The report on "policies and procedures of the Forensic Division of St. Elizabeths Hospital" included in its lengthy 104 pages (excluding appendices) a statement of the panel's belief that "more than mental illness must be addressed in calibrating the extent of a patient's recovery and suitability for release under a particular set of circumstances."[43] Recognizing the absence of any valid and reliable formula for assessing the dangerousness of either "mentally ill" or "nonmentally ill" persons, the report lamely recommended that "rules need to be developed about what information is clinically relevant to the assessment and treatment process." Such information should be released to attorneys on both sides of the issue at the same time, the report continued, adding that "if there is any doubt as to the relevance of certain information to the court's determination, the Hospital should resolve the doubt in favor of disclosure."[44]

The following summer the hospital once again recommended a release for John Hinckley, and once again it found itself shocked and embarrassed about what it didn't know about its most notorious patient. In July the hospital proposed a day of escorted "therapeutic recreational activity" off hospital grounds. Shortly after the court and government attorneys were presented with the request the Secret Service produced a letter Hinckley had written to a mail-order house requesting a nude drawing of Jodie Foster. Having lost his collection of photographs of Foster the year before, when his room was searched, a determined Hinckley would now settle for a drawing. It was obvious

that six years of treatment had had little effect on the obsession that had prompted—his own attorney had once
argued—his attempt on the president's life.

The mail-order house notified the Secret Service soon after the letter arrived.[45] When the hospital was informed, it
immediately withdrew its second release request, as it had
the first. Also for the second time it did so on the basis of
information pressed forward by government attorneys
rather than by its own doctors.

Hinckley's attorneys did the only thing they could do,
filing a petition to have this new damaging information
sealed, arguing that Hinckley's "privacy and property interests" would be violated if the contents of his mail were
made public.[46] Like the story on Hinckley's photographs,
this one about a nude drawing, too, was leaked. On August 26 the *Washington Post* published a story revealing the
substance of Hinckley's mail-order request.

Once again troubling questions arose concerning St.
Elizabeths' treatment and management procedures. Hinckley's doctors seemed too easily swayed by the *words* of
this manipulative young man. There was obviously little
awareness of what he was actually *doing*. Was Hinckley de-
ceiving his doctors, faking a recovery in much the same
way that prosecutors believed he had faked the extent of
his illness during his trial?

Hinckley's mental disorder had always defied textbook
classification. The hospital's 1982 Bolton Report had had
this to say about Hinckley's condition: "All conference
members agree that he *cannot* be classified easily under the
criteria of DSM-III. He clearly satisfies the established criteria of some diagnostic categories (e.g., narcissistic personality disorder). However, the symptomatology does not al-
low us to place him in any one category without feeling that
we are either over-diagnosing or under-diagnosing."[47]

It was beginning to look to some as if Hinckley's "narcissistic personality disorder" was simply one dimension
of a multidimensional sociopathic personality. His impul-
siveness, his poor judgment, his inability to learn from

mistakes, and his shrewd dishonesty—not to mention his propensity for violence—all pointed to the absence of conscience that is the hallmark of the sociopath.

But was he still dangerous? And what constitutes clinically relevant information in assessments of a person's potential for violence? Unfortunately no one is sure. Dr. Turkus believed that the Bundy letters were not significant enough to mention, while government attorneys saw the correspondence as a familiar extension of Hinckley's well-documented fascination with violence.

Assessing dangerousness isn't based on scientific expertise, a doctor at St. Elizabeths admitted defensively. It's based only on a "gut" feeling. "In the end it comes down to the guts of a psychiatrist," he said, "and the guts of a judge."[48]

PART II

Chapter Five

THE SOCIOPATHIC PERSPECTIVE: HINCKLEY, BREMER, AND MASS MURDERERS

WHETHER or not John Hinckley was—and remains—insane is a question that will be debated for a long time by those who disagreed with his jury's verdict. But that, as we have seen, is no longer the real issue. Whatever the state of Hinckley's mind, there can be little doubt that, like other assassins and would-be assassins before him, he was—and remains—a very dangerous person. More specifically Hinckley fits the behavioral pattern of a Type III sociopathic assassin.

In earlier research I suggested that all but two American assassins fall into four basic motivational patterns that span the distance between rational political extremism, through various degrees of emotional disturbance, to outright insanity.[1] Before 1963 American assassins were usually either rational political extremists or utterly insane. In the former category, which I labeled Type I subjects, I placed John Wilkes Booth, President Lincoln's assassin in 1865; Leon Czolgosz, President McKinley's assassin in 1901; and Oscar Collazo and Griselio Torresola, President Truman's would-be assassins in 1950. Those I considered to be insane were Richard Lawrence, President Jackson's attacker in 1835; Charles Guiteau, President Garfield's assassin in 1881; and John Schrank, presidential candidate Theodore Roosevelt's attacker in 1912. The two exceptions to the pattern in this earlier era were the atypical assassin, Dr. Carl Weiss, who killed Senator Huey Long in 1935, and Giuseppe Zangara, an emotionally disturbed (Type III) Italian immigrant who, in his attempt on President Franklin D.

Roosevelt's life in 1933, killed Chicago Mayor Anton Cermak.

Beginning in 1963, the year television coverage raised the drama of assassination to an unprecedented level, the pattern changed. Six of the eight attacks upon presidents or other national political figures in this later era have been carried out by emotionally disturbed, but sane, persons—sane, that is, by the standards of the M'Naghten rule, which is to say that each of the six knew what he or she was doing, and all were also aware of the legal consequences. In addition to Lee Harvey Oswald, who killed President Kennedy in 1963, the five others who fit this description are: Arthur Bremer who shot presidential candidate Governor George Wallace in 1972; Samuel Byck, who tried to crash-dive a jetliner into the Nixon White House in 1974; Lynette Fromme and Sara Jane Moore, who made separate attempts on President Ford's life in 1975; and, the most recent, John Hinckley in 1981. All six conform to the closely related patterns of emotionally disturbed subjects I have labeled Type II and Type III. There are only two exceptions in this period: James Earl Ray, Martin Luther King, Jr.'s, atypical assassin in 1968—the only contract assassin in American history; and, two months later, the Palestinian assassin Sirhan Sirhan, who was acting as a rational political extremist when he killed presidential candidate Senator Robert Kennedy.

In this chapter I will begin by discussing the general defining characteristics of the Type II and Type III categories first formulated in 1982.[2] Then I will narrow that focus to the Type III category, using Bremer and Hinckley as examples. The chapter will conclude with a discussion of how the Type III characteristics are shared by a number of mass murderers.

DEFINITIONS: TYPE II AND TYPE III SUBJECTS

A Type II or III subject is a person with overwhelming and aggressive egocentric needs for acceptance, recognition, and status which have been denied or withdrawn by those persons he has needed most—usually some combination of parents and spouses, or other persons whom he is strongly attracted to or dependent upon. The subject's already profound feelings of inadequacy, the sources of which can be traced back to childhood, leave him poorly prepared to cope with such searing disappointments. He possesses neither the coping skills nor other necessary resources to deal with the hurt, frustration, and anger that eventually consume him. Seeing no way out of his difficulties, he becomes suicidal. Like many suicides, he sees dying as a way of getting back at those he blames for his unhappiness. Unlike most ordinary suicides, who internalize their aggression, the Type II or III subject displaces, or redirects, part of his, selecting surrogate victims to die with him.

Type II and Type III subjects share a driving need to be noticed and to control others. It is that quality which sets them apart from ordinary suicides. And that, of course, is why they act publicly and include other prominent victims. People far removed from the real difficulties of the Type II and III subjects' lives become surrogate victims in their tragic schemes because of the attention such victims will focus on them. Also present is a compelling desire to express, in the most visible manner possible, the anger and resentment that consumes them.

The two types differ in their reasons for selecting particular victims. Type II subjects need scapegoats to blame for their disappointing lives. Thus victims are selected because of their political views, even though those views are clearly secondary to the Type II subject's real personal motives. But those motives are invariably rationalized in political terms. For example, would-be assassin Samuel Byck's painstaking effort to explain his attempt on President Nixon's life as something he was doing to rid the country of political corruption was in reality a vain attempt to rationalize a suicide decision precipitated by an unwanted divorce.[a]

[a] Similarly, one can only guess what Lee Harvey Oswald would have said had he lived. But his previous activities suggest that it would be reasonable to assume that a political rationale would have been offered.

Type III assassins choose their political victims because of their prominence and visibility, *not* their political views. Political purpose has nothing to do with the Type III subjects' actions. For that reason nonpolitical persons of comparable celebrity status could serve the same objective.[b] Type III subjects do not blame their surrogate victims for their problems, nor do they feel any more animosity toward them than they do toward most of society. Their estrangement is complete. They make no attempt to attach any ideological or altruistic meaning to their actions. The reason for this is that Type III subjects are not constrained by conscience. Their acts are simply the expression of a perverse rage that consumes them—nothing more. There is no need to justify; there is also no sense of remorse. Guilt and remorse, for the Type III personality are unfamiliar atrophied emotions. Consider, for example, that Arthur Bremer's (Type III) explanation for why he shot Governor Wallace was a sneering denial of politics and of purpose. "Ask me why I did it," Bremer wrote, "and I'd say, 'I don't know,' or 'Nothing else to do,' or 'Why not?' or 'I have to kill somebody.' "[3] Hinckley's frivolous explanation for shooting President Reagan was equally devoid of political meaning. "I shot Reagan to prove my love for Jodie Foster," he told *Penthouse* magazine in 1983, "and [to] try to impress her with my historical deed."[4]

Another way of describing this difference between Type II and Type III subjects is to say that the Type III subject has hit the bottom of that lacerating emotional slide toward complete estrangement and alienation, while the Type II is still sliding, with the last remnants of conscience reflected in the need to rationalize and justify his suicidal act.[c] Type III subjects like Arthur Bremer and John Hinckley had hit that bottom. No such need existed. There was no political

[b] Mark David Chapman's senseless murder of rock superstar John Lennon in 1980 provides a case in point.

[c] These differences in *degree*, however, should not obscure the differences in *kind* that distinguish these emotionally disturbed subjects from the truly politically motivated assassin, on the one hand, and the truly insane, on the other. But the fact remains that, since 1963, the emotionally

justification, no scapegoating, no rationalization, and only the flimsiest of explanations. But what is the source of this perversity?

TYPE III SOCIALIZATION PATTERNS: BREMER AND HINCKLEY

The key to the personalities of both Arthur Bremer and John Hinckley is that both grew up with great anxieties about being loved and wanted.[d] The seeds of these fears were sown in early childhood and were brought to full bloom by the bitter disappointments experienced during early adulthood. By that time, estranged from their families and rejected by young women they hardly knew, both felt that they were *unlovable*.

Recall from the previous chapters the parental conflict and difficulties John Hinckley experienced as a child. These difficulties that marked him for life were the result of the Hinckley family chemistry: most notably, a distant and demanding father who, probably because he himself had been raised without a father's love, was as poorly prepared to understand his own son's need for it as he was to express it. And he was often absent. John Hinckley grew up never having learned to love, and to be loved, as a man. At the other extreme his mother was an anxious, frequently intimidated woman who, with the best intentions, appeared to cling too closely, too long, to her baby son and, in the process, passed on to him many of her own fears, reinforcing values and behavior that had made him a wimpish social misfit by his teenage years. At twenty-five John Hinckley was a young man who was too fearful to drive in city traffic or at night and whose mother still selected the clothes he wore. By that time even she didn't want this

---

disturbed assassin poses a bigger security threat than either his truly political or truly insane counterparts. Only the threat of international terrorism looms larger.

[d]Although the pattern is the same, the third Type III subject, Giuseppe Zangara, is omitted from this discussion. Fewer specifics are known about Zangara's troubled background.

excessively dependent whiner around, and he knew it. The forced departure that he had always feared was a shattering experience. A few years later, when Jodie Foster made it clear that she didn't want him around either, John Hinckley began stalking the president.

Bremer's story is somewhat different, but the results are the same. A social worker described Bremer's mother, Sylvia, as a suspicious, withdrawn woman who had been raised in an orphanage after her mother had abandoned her. Consumed by the fears that grew out of that experience, she trusted no one, including her husband. Bremer's father, Bill, relied on the bottle to insulate himself from the hostile outbursts that regularly punctuated the silences of the household. Mr. Bremer never got mean when he drank; he never mistreated his children. He just got quiet. That was what he was much of the time—a benign nonentity who went to work, brought home his pay, skirmished with his wife, and often slept in a chair.

Bremer's two older brothers and an older sister left home as teenagers to escape the tension and conflict. When they did, his mother compensated by focusing her attention on this blond cherubic little boy who rarely did anything to annoy her. But the care she gave him was completely lacking in warmth and communication as little Artie was subjected to ritualistic forms of attention, all to prove that the older children were wrong, that this anxious, obsessive woman was a "good mother."[5] Bremer was toilet-trained early, for example, by being placed on a cold toilet seat every half hour. As a social worker put it, Arthur was "fed, toileted, clothed on some impersonal, extraneous schedule and never fondled or talked to." It showed. Bremer became a compliant little boy who rarely cried and, in fact, didn't say a word until he was four years old.[6]

Bremer's adolescence was much like Hinckley's in some important respects. He played sports one year and quit; he had few friends, no school activities, and mediocre grades, in spite of above-average intelligence. Like Hinckley, Bremer never dated in high school. It wasn't that neither one wanted to—they did. It was because neither of these pleasant-looking but painfully shy and inhibited boys had learned how to socialize with women on a mature level. Women, except for their mothers, were strangers. As they reached adulthood, both Bremer and Hinckley had the social and sexual sophistication of thirteen-year-olds.

Bremer's understanding of sex came from the "sex comics" he purchased from mail-order houses and his mother's intrusive interest in his "intimate bodily functions." When asked how the facts of life were explained to Arthur, his mother replied proudly, "He never asked, and he was always clean [meaning he never masturbated]." She never encouraged him to date as he grew older, warning that the "oppressive odors of menstruating girls" in crowded high school classrooms contributed to his frequent headaches. When Bremer began his senior year in high school, Sylvia was still checking his sheets and keeping track of how often he changed his underwear, as if he were a child.[7]

In a different and less bizarre manner John Hinckley was also treated too long as if he were a child. But, unlike Bremer, Hinckley wanted that. Until he discovered Jodie Foster, his mother seems to have been the only woman he ever truly wanted in his life. As a result of this strong, unresolved—some would say Oedipal—attraction, he denied his sexuality, cloaking it in Victorian romanticism, claiming wonderment over why people (like Bremer) were so interested in sex.

Thus the symmetry of the mother-son relationships differed—an obsessively controlling mother, in Bremer's case; an excessively dependent son, in Hinckley's—but the results were the same. Neither boy entered adulthood prepared to function on a mature level with women because neither had developed a positive, cohesive sense of his own maleness during adolescence. And for the same reasons neither had developed a mature conception of personal responsibility that we associate with conscience. They remained immature, irresponsible little boys unprepared to channel their sexual desires in a normal fashion.

Similarly, neither boy had learned how to deal appropriately with normal feelings of frustration and hostility. Initially their responses were simply withdrawal and suppression. But the resulting social isolation only made matters worse. As the resentment toward their parents began to grow and fester, it found different expressions. Unlike the moody, passive aggression—focused on his father—that began in Hinckley's adolescence, Bremer's anger—focused on his mother—didn't emerge until his senior year of high school; then it was direct. At that time the previously quiet, obedient Arthur began to complain about his mother's cooking and to argue with his father over trivial matters. Then, in a complete turnabout, this compulsively neat and "clean" boy began to leave soiled clothing and pornographic comics scattered about his room. It was plain that Arthur wanted his mother to find what she had been snooping around looking for as long as he could remember.

Bremer's employment and educational history closely resembles Hinckley's. After high school graduation Bremer worked sporadically for three years as a busboy and at other menial jobs. He also took a few courses in writing, psychology, art, and photography at Milwaukee Technical College, but he failed to complete most of them. It is the events of this period of his life that screenwriter Paul Schrader drew upon for *Taxi Driver*. While working as a janitor at an elementary school, Bremer fell in love with a fifteen-year-old hall monitor. He began to plan excitedly for his first romance. But like Hinckley with his futile forays to New Haven, Bremer was poorly prepared for a relationship, and his expectations were equally unrealistic.

Soon after he met the girl, he left home and moved to his own apartment, mainly to get away from his mother. But it was difficult. Sylvia continued to call during the night to see if he was in; she would also stop by his apartment at odd hours to check on him, perhaps to see if anyone else was there. Bremer, at twenty-one, was still trying to escape his mother's assaults on his privacy.[8] By this time he had grown to hate this cold, disapproving, domineering woman, much as John Hinckley was growing—at the same time, far to the south in Dallas—to hate his father for many of the same reasons.

Unlike Hinckley with his tepid emotions—the mushy notes and whimpering phone calls that worked on his mother but not on Jodie Foster—Bremer was looking for hot, sweaty, gymnastic sex of the kind depicted in the sex comics he read and masturbated with. It was obvious that neither Bremer nor Hinckley had learned much about sex from his father. There was little communication of any kind between father and son in either family, let alone on awkward subjects. Neither boy saw his father as a role model. Hinckley despised the domineering Jack; Bremer was contemptuous of the boozy Bill.

In this developmental void Bremer came to believe that the way to the young girl's heart was through the dirty pictures he showed her on their first date, spiced with the vulgar language he thought she would find sexually stimulating. His approach was reflected on screen in *Taxi Driver*, as an amusingly naive Travis Bickle, making the same assumption about women, escorts a respectable young woman he barely knows to a grainy porno film on their first date. Bremer's young date and her girlfriends were offended and embarrassed by his clumsy immaturity. Although she had at first been impressed by the attention of this "older man," Bremer's fifteen-year-old quickly broke off the relationship. Bremer responded by shaving his head, buying a gun, and beginning to think seriously about killing other people and himself, just as Travis Bickle did in the film based, in part, on Bremer's life.

At this time his reading list expanded beyond sex comics to include many of the same books on assassins that John Hinckley would read seven or eight years later—among them *R.F.K. Must Die!* by Robert Blair Kaiser, and *Sirhan* by Aziz Shihab. (In fact, after reading *Sirhan*, Bremer called Shihab and, identifying himself only as "Art," asked him if a person is justified in murdering another "if his love fails, or his girlfriend jilts him." When Shihab suggested to his caller that he had misread the book, Bremer became angry and hung up.)[9]

PSYCHOLOGICAL LINKS: BREMER AND HINCKLEY

Despite the vast socioeconomic distance that separates Arthur Bremer and John Hinckley—one the son of a marginally employed Milwaukee truck driver, the other the son of a millionaire Denver oilman—their personalities and certain aspects of their lives are remarkably similar. These similarities are significant not only because Hinckley read Bremer's published diary,[10] but also, as I have just indicated, because the film *Taxi Driver* draws heavily from the same source in developing certain important dimensions of its main character, Travis Bickle. While much was made at Hinckley's trial of his attempts to imitate—or, as defense psychiatrists argued, to *become*—the fictional Travis Bickle, there was no mention of his close behavioral resemblance to the real-life would-be assassin Bremer.[e] The primary difference between Bremer and the Bickle character drawn from his life was that Bremer didn't meet an Iris among any of the New York prostitutes whom he, like John Hinckley, visited after his true love rejected him.

There can be little doubt that Hinckley admired violent criminals and identified with them. Following this path of what some have called "negative" identities, or role models, it is tempting to suggest that life creates art as Bremer gives life to the fictional Bickle; then life imitates art as Hinckley, in turn, sees *Taxi Driver* and chooses Bickle as a surrogate role model—a belated substitute for the father he couldn't stand. To do so, however, one must ignore the

[e]Hinckley's curiosity didn't end with Bremer's diary. The following articles were found in his Evergreen bedroom after his arrest: "Wallace Shot," *Dallas Morning News*, May 16, 1972; "Did America Shoot Wallace?" *Time* (no date); and "The Wallace Shooting," *Life*, May 26, 1972.

direct link between Hinckley and Bremer through Bremer's diary. Was the role model really Travis Bickle, or was it in fact Arthur Bremer?

There is a long list of similarities between Hinckley and Bremer: the submissive personalities; the social isolation; the indifferent performance in school; the family conflict; the early preoccupation with suicide; the menial jobs and aimless existence, despite above-average intelligence; the eventual family estrangement; the failed first romance with a very young girl (or, in Hinckley's case, a young woman whose screen image was that of a much younger person); the interest in handguns and violence that followed; the sexual initiation rites with prostitutes, far from home, in New York; the great impression film depictions of violence had on both; the various options of suicide and mass murder each considered before choosing assassination; the intense interest each had in previous assassins; the manner in which the victim was selected on the basis of popularity rather than politics; the stalking behavior that followed; and, finally, the diaries and other writings each kept.[11]

Some of these similarities could have occurred by chance, but the overall pattern cannot be dismissed as mere coincidence. Neither can the Bremer-Hinckley similarities that exist on a deeper psychological level.

But who would they kill, and how? Bremer, like Hinckley, couldn't decide. While in the midst of this indecision, Bremer saw a film that made a lasting impression—Stanley Kubrick's *A Clockwork Orange*. As he admitted in his diary, Bremer began "fantasizing myself as the Alek on the screen." The Alek he was referring to is the film's main character, played by Malcolm McDowell, a young man completely alienated from British society who decides to strike back by destroying representatives of that society in the most sadistic manner possible. After first considering a mass murder in his hometown, Bremer decided that assassinating a prominent representative of that "silent majority" would be a more spectacular, more outrageously perverse act. His first choice was President Nixon; he settled for Governor Wallace.[12]

This link between Alek and Arthur was the first of the links in a chain of violence that would eventually include not only Alek and Arthur but also as I have suggested, Arthur and Travis and finally Travis and John. But neither of the real-life links in this chain had members of the English upper class to torture as Alek did in *A Clockwork Orange* nor pimps to kill as Travis did at the bloody conclusion of *Taxi Driver*. Instead, George Wallace and Ronald Reagan would pay the price for their bitter alienation and hostility.[13]

Type III Assassins and Mass Murderers

The perverse, displaced rage of the Type III subjects Arthur Bremer and John Hinckley also resembles, as I have mentioned, that of certain mass murderers. Both assassination and mass murder ensure notoriety and a semblance of dominance or control for the killers. It is probably not mere coincidence that both assassination attempts and mass murders have increased dramatically since 1963.

Like assassinations, mass murders ensure that the killer's actions will have page-one significance, if not meaning. Both crimes represent final raging statements about a society that had no place for their perpetrators. It is also no mere coincidence that the Type III subjects Bremer and Hinckley considered mass murder and suicide before selecting political victims instead.[f] Before shooting Governor Wallace, Bremer considered hijacking an armored truck, parking it in a busy Milwaukee intersection, and then shooting as many people as possible from its slit win-

---

[f] Less is known about the personal life of the third Type III assassin, Giuseppe Zangara, who was executed in 1933. Although his bitter estrangement from his family and a "dirty capitalist" society was complete, it is not known whether Zangara, like Bremer and Hinckley, considered mass murder.

dows.[14] Hinckley, as we know, considered a mass shooting on the Yale campus and a similar event in the chambers of the U.S. Senate.

The reverse is also true: some mass murderers were potential assassins. According to the wife of mass murderer James Huberty, her extremely bitter husband was a potential assassin. Before Huberty's 1984 rampage at a San Ysidro McDonald's Restaurant where he killed twenty-one people, President Jimmy Carter was the person he blamed for the loss of his job and investments, and Carter was usually the subject of his verbal tirades.[15] Sniper Mark Jimmy Essex, who was killed in 1973 on the roof of the Howard Johnson's hotel in New Orleans after murdering six people, had an apartment with walls plastered with political slogans, among them "Kill pig Nixon and all his running dogs" and "Political power comes from the barrel of a gun."[16] And one can only wonder about those Midwestern farmers who, while blaming federal farm policy, sometimes kill their families and other times their bankers when they can't make the payments on their loans. That threat is something the Secret Service thought about a lot, a few years ago, on presidential trips into the troubled heartland of America.

Moreover, there are striking similarities between the background characteristics of Type III subjects and those of mass murderers. The authors of one of the few comparative studies of mass murders conclude that the killers are usually marginally employed, socially isolated, white males who have recently endured some frustrating event(s), such as a loss of employment or the rejection of someone important to them.[17] These characteristics are identical to those observed in the Type III subjects Bremer and Hinckley.

In the same study of mass murder the authors state that in 75 percent of the 364 cases they studied the killers knew their victims.[18] The motives of mass murderers who know their victims, and are expressing their hostility directly, are usually easier to identify. Often the victims are family members or fellow employees.[g] The choice of victims is selective, not random.[h] And in virtually every case there is some frustration, some grievance, that has developed between the killer and his victims which precedes the tragedy.

But it is the remaining 25 percent of mass murderers, those who select their victims *randomly*—who kill strangers—that come closest to having the bizarre, nihilistic motives of the Type III assassin. For example, in addition to James Huberty and Mark Essex, Charles Whitman shot forty-four people, killing thirteen, from his perch in the University of Texas tower in 1966. In 1984, five months after James Huberty's rampage in San Ysidro, Michael Feher barricaded himself atop the stadium at the University of

---

[g]For example, in 1987 alone there were at least three such incidents: a former Air Force sergeant killed fourteen members of his family in Arkansas; another man killed his parents, in-laws, wife, and two children in the state of Washington; and another man gunned down seven relatives in Missouri. Only the Air Force sergeant survived.

Similar instances of occupational frustration being expressed in mass bloodshed are regularly reported. For example, in 1976 a man in Baltimore, angry because of delays in receiving a business permit, shot five municipal employees, killing one; in 1982 an IBM salesman shot five fellow workers, killing three, because he felt that he had been passed over for promotion; in 1986 a disgruntled postal employee in Oklahoma killed fourteen fellow employees before taking his own life; and in 1987 a recently dismissed airline employee shot a pilot, his former boss, and himself, causing the crash of a Pacific Southwestern flight that, incidentally, killed forty other passengers.

[h] Mass murderers should not be confused with serial murderers, like Ted Bundy and Henry Lee Lucas, for example, who kill repeatedly over time. There are significant differences between the two groups in motivation as well as in the choice of victims. Unlike mass murderers, serial murderers are not suicidal; they carefully execute their crimes to avoid arrest. Often the recurrent nature of their violence has a sexual basis. Finally, the serial killer carefully selects his victims, usually on the basis of some combination of physical characteristics, most frequently sex, age, and appearance (for example, hair color, race, and ethnicity), whereas mass murderers are indifferent to such considerations, selecting as victims anyone unlucky enough to stray into their sights.

Oregon and shot two people, killing one of them before he was killed. In 1989 another troubled young man, Patrick Edward Purdy, opened fire on a schoolyard full of children in Stockton, California, with an AK-47 assault rifle; he wounded thirty and killed five before he killed himself. And there are others. All the killers mentioned died at the scene, as they intended to do, their motives remaining obscure.

Such people kill, it seems—like Type III assassins—simply to make a statement about their disillusionment with their own lives. They also resemble Type III subjects in that most did not appear to be psychotic. Angry, yes, but not mad.[i] Neither the Type III assassin nor the *anonymous* mass murderer is inhibited by conscience, nor is he constrained by fear. Fear has little meaning to a person who wants to die. Such people have lost their regard for human life in large part because their own frustrating lives are so awful. A poem John Hinckley wrote reflects the perversity of this theme:

> I remain the mortal enemy of Man
> I can't escape this torture chamber
> I can't begin to be happy
> I plot revenge in the dark
> I plot escape from this asylum
> I follow the example of perverts.[19]

There are other similarities. Like the Type III assassin, the anonymous mass murderer selects surrogate targets, instead of actual targets, for his rage. In other words, un-

---

[i] After Charles Whitman's rampage at the University of Texas an autopsy revealed a malignant tumor "the size of a pecan" on his brain that may have triggered his actions. Other evidence, primarily Whitman's diary and the notes of the psychiatrist who was treating him, suggest that he had thought about the attack for some time and was fully aware of what he was doing. Careful planning and preparation had preceded the shooting. See Walter Sullivan, "Effects of a Tumor on the Brain Can Cause Antisocial Behavior," and Paul L. Montgomery, "Sniper Told About Deaths in Note 'To Whom It May Concern'," *New York Times*, August 3, 1966, p. 20.

like a family or workplace killer, the anonymous mass murderer is not motivated by anything his chosen victims have done to him; rather, it is what his victims *represent*, or symbolize in his mind, that focuses the diffuse anger and rage of his attack. His alienation has spread like an infection, poisoning his perspective on life, draining away whatever compassion and humanity he might have had. Like Bremer's and Hinckley's, his estrangement is so complete that suicide alone simply isn't sufficient to express the unmet dependency needs, the unchanneled sexual drives, that fuel the ulcerating anger and frustration eating away within. Another Hinckley poem conveys the feeling:

> A solitary weed among carnations
> The last living shit on earth
> Dracula on a crowded beach
> A child without a home
> The loser of a one-man race . . .[20]

In a motivational sense it is that desire to be noticed—even as a "weed among carnations"—that the anonymous mass killer also shares with the Type III assassin. To "make a statement," to be "taken seriously" for once in his miserable, pointless life is the goal. And accompanying that desire to be noticed is a desperate need to dominate, to be in control. A violent rampage through the bedrooms of one's home or the corridors of one's place of employment isn't sufficient. What he wants is a truly commanding public event, an act so vile, so out of proportion, that it will be remembered—in part because it will be televised, as most momentous public events have been since 1963.[j] Television alone ensures that his name, and his deed, and his contempt will be etched in the public memory just as Lee Harvey Oswald's and Sirhan Sirhan's were. For a person who

[j] Since that time not only has Secret Service protection steadily increased but television cameras record the president's every movement outside the White House. At scenes of ordinary, everyday violence, television crews, attuned to police scanners, frequently arrive before ambulances.

has struggled a lifetime with his feelings of insignificance and worthlessness it is heady stuff—a spectacular and enduring epitaph. As Arthur Bremer put it before he shot Wallace: "Hey world! Come here! I wanna talk to ya! If I don't kill—if I don't kill myself I want you to pay through the nose, ears, & belly button. . . . when I kill Wallace, I hope everyone screams & hollers and everything!! I hope the rally goes mad!!! The silent majority will be my benefactor in the biggest hijack ever!"[21] After his arrest John Hinckley was more restrained: "I was desperate in some bold way," he explained, "to get . . . attention."[22]

Thus for his victims the killer selects either people of prominence or a sufficient number of ordinary people to make the event newsworthy—the cover of *Newsweek* rather than the column in the local newspaper that an ordinary murder-suicide would garner him. In the killer's mind both kinds of victims symbolize the hated society. Their death gives him the same exhilarating sense of power that a hunter feels when he kills a dangerous beast, for to this outcast society is that beast. The number of mass murders exceeds those of assassinations in part simply because ordinary people provide more accessible targets; but for some like Bremer and Hinckley, those with the patience to stalk and wait, the real trophies are powerful political personalities.

Such symbols may change as the killer reevaluates the status of his intended victim(s). Arthur Bremer's decision to kill the ultraconservative George Wallace was shaken when he read that Wallace's liberal rival for the Democratic nomination, George McGovern, was improving in the polls. "The whole country's going liberal. I can see it in McGovern," he wrote angrily in his diary. "You know my biggest failure may be when I kill Wallace."[23] But as Bremer also noted in his diary, it was Wallace who was claiming to represent the "Silent Majority" of an American society against which Bremer sought revenge—and opinion polls Bremer consulted eventually confirmed that he was right. McGovern's appeals to young people, women, and minorities cost him the election, but it may have saved his life. In Bremer's final twisted analysis it was a choice between randomly killing members of Wallace's "Silent Majority" as they crowded a Milwaukee intersection or killing the candidate they favored.[24]

Recall that John Hinckley went through the same kind of reevaluation before he decided to shoot President Reagan. Sensing the probability of President Carter's defeat in the November election, he stopped his stalk of Carter to await his replacement. And we will never know for sure what calculations ran through the minds of Mark Essex, James Huberty, and other mass murderers. With Essex and Huberty it may have been simply that Richard Nixon and Jimmy Carter were far away in Washington the day the mood hit them, and there were all those folks around the Howard Johnson's hotel and inside the McDonald's restaurant close by, right there in the neighborhood.

Official concern and scholarly curiosity about the threat posed by such dangerous persons as Whitman, Bremer, Essex, Hinckley, and Huberty has increased in recent years as the tragic events with which they are associated continue to occur with disturbing regularity. The Hinckley case illustrates that assessing dangerousness is an even more difficult assignment when the subject is a sociopath. Sociopaths, like Hinckley, are often intelligent, manipulative, and charmingly deceptive when they want to be. As the controversy surrounding the management of his case at St. Elizabeths Hospital reveals, a sociopath will tell a person anything that suits his purposes. Unrestrained by conscience or guilt, a sociopath gives verbal assurances that mean little. It is a wonder that Hinckley's doctors continue to place so much stock in what he tells them about himself.

A search continues in the behavioral sciences to discover better methods to sort through the cluster of background, behavioral, and personality characteristics that might identify such dangerous people before they strike. It is to those efforts that I now turn.

Chapter Six

PREDICTING DANGEROUSNESS: ACTUARIAL AND CLINICAL APPROACHES

THE CONTROVERSY that characterizes John Hinckley's attempts to gain early release is not unusual; it's just that Hinckley's much-sought-after notoriety puts it on the front page of newspapers. Just as Hinckley's acquittal raised questions about the scientific basis of insanity pleas, so are other equally important questions raised about the ability of mental health professionals to predict dangerousness. Like diagnosing insanity, predicting dangerousness remains an art, not a science, and an imperfect one at that. My purpose in this chapter is twofold. First I will examine Hinckley in a comparative historical perspective with other assassins and would-be assassins; then, drawing on this perspective, I will suggest why the methods used for assessing the danger posed by people like Hinckley lead to controversy. It is a perspective that will focus on potential assassins but, for the reasons suggested earlier, it may also be helpful in identifying potential public mass murderers.

In my previous work on American assassins I studied the sixteen people responsible for these earlier attacks.[1] John Hinckley was added to the list while the book was in press, but he was not, for obvious reasons, included in the original work. I suggested a typology of assassins and would-be assassins that was derived from an assessment of dispositional and contextual factors. That typology is summarized in Chart 1. The subjects, as I have indicated earlier, ranged from rational political extremists (Type I), through two shades of mental and emotional disturbance (Type II and Type III), to the truly insane (Type IV). The distribution of subjects is presented in Chart 2.

CHART 1
Types of American Assassins

Characteristics	Type I	Type II	Type III	Type IV
Emotional distortion	Mild	Moderate	Severe	Severe
Cognitive distortion	Absent	Absent	Absent	Severe
Hallucinations	Absent	Absent	Absent	Present
Delusions	Absent	Absent	Absent	Present
Reality contact	Clear	Clear	Clear	Poor
Social relations	Varied	Disturbed	Isolated	Isolated
Primary motive	Political	Personal/ Compensatory	Personal/ Provocation	Irrational

Source: This and the following figure are drawn from *American Assassins: The Darker Side of Politics* (Princeton, N.J.: Princeton University Press, 1982), pp. 260 and 17, respectively.

CHART 2
Classification of American Assassins and Would-Be Assassins
(1835–1981)

Rational———————Disturbed—————————Irrational			
Type I	Type II	Type III	Type IV
Booth	Oswald	Zangara	Lawrence
Czolgosz	Byck	Bremer	Guiteau
Collazo	Fromme	Hinckley	Schrank
Torresola	Moore		
Sirhan			

Atypical
Weiss
Ray

This relatively small number of only seventeen actual subjects contrasts sharply with the over 26,000 persons who have been investigated by the Secret Service as being potential threats to the president (or other persons in their charge) and the 250 to 400 suspects, drawn from that total, who at any one time are considered dangerous and placed on the Service's "watch list" for "Quarterly Investigation" (QI Subjects) and protective surveillance.[2] There are tough decisions to make. The president's life depends on them being made correctly—not to mention that there are constitutional and legal implications of improper arrests—and the decisions are still based largely on the intuition of Secret Service agents; it is a "very difficult and subjective problem for case agents."[3] No one knows how actual assassins differ from the thousands of nondangerous subjects who are brought to the attention of the Secret Service, or the hundreds of those considered dangerous and marked for quarterly investigation. How does one distinguish between the real threats and the bluffs? Between a Lee Harvey Oswald, for example, who only ten days before he killed President Kennedy threatened to bomb the FBI's Dallas office, and a harmless drunk who, referring to the president, says somebody ought to shoot the so-and-so? The FBI apparently assumed that Oswald fit into the latter category.[a]

It is a difficult problem for the Secret Service agents assigned to the sixty-three field offices across the country who must shoulder the bulk of this responsibility. There are no formulas to gauge the seriousness of the threat posed; there is no checklist of symptoms, no valid profile of characteristics to go by; and there are no mental health pro-

---

[a] Another possible reason the FBI may have failed to follow up on Oswald's threat, as it was required to do, is that an FBI agent's interest in his wife Marina had perhaps evolved into something more than official curiosity, as Oswald charged at the time. The follow-up investigation that Oswald warranted may have been deliberately *avoided* simply because the agent did not want to confront an angry husband whose suspicions about the agent's actual intentions were justified.

fessionals to call upon who are any better prepared to evaluate dangerousness of this kind than experienced Secret Service agents themselves.[4]

There is probably little to distinguish between suspects and actual assassins in actuarial and clinical terms.[b] Fifty-four percent of the people who come to the attention of the Secret Service as possible threats to protected persons have a history of mental illness.[5] As Chart 2 indicates, 59 percent of the actual assassins and would-be assassins (ten of the seventeen) can be so described. Yet one suspects that real assassins are, in some very important way, different.

Although I emphasized the importance of context in my earlier work on assassins and would-be assassins, I did not define with any operational rigor what elements within those contexts were of critical importance. But despite these operational and predictive limitations, the typology described in *American Assassins* represents a significant departure from the view of American assassins described in the earlier literature. That earlier body of work missed important motivational distinctions among assassins because it failed to take into account the varying political contexts of their acts. Considered in this contextual vacuum, it is hardly surprising that assassins as different as John Wilkes Booth and Charles Guiteau were both "diagnosed" as paranoid schizophrenics.[6] This presumption of mental illness may also be reflected in the Secret Service's report that "95 percent of those individuals considered dangerous to protected persons had some kind of contact with the mental health sector."[7] A telling statistic? Or might one ask in this secular age of counseling and therapy, who among those who can afford it hasn't?

Perhaps it is for this reason that law enforcement agencies (including the FBI and the Secret Service, as well as local police) which drew upon such flawed research for guidance have questioned and released as insufficient

[b] This statement cannot be made with complete certainty since the investigative files of the Secret Service are closed.

threats five of the last eight persons who have attacked American presidents. Lee Harvey Oswald, for example, was well known to the FBI before he killed President Kennedy in 1963; Samuel Byck had been interviewed three times by the Secret Service before his attempt on President Nixon's life in 1974; Lynette Fromme's threats were known to both the FBI and local police before her 1975 attack on President Ford; Sara Jane Moore was well known to the FBI,[c] had hinted at her intentions to local law enforcement officials, and was interviewed by the Secret Service the night before she fired a shot at President Ford, also in 1975; and an armed John Hinckley was arrested and released by local authorities at the Nashville airport in 1980—the same day Carter was scheduled to arrive in Nashville. One might also include Arthur Bremer, whose conspicuous attire and behavior were observed by authorities at a number of George Wallace's campaign rallies in 1972—days, and hundreds of miles, apart—before he finally got close enough to cripple the governor and wound one of his bodyguards in the parking lot of a Maryland shopping center. Was it because none of these subjects seemed to be sufficiently disturbed to warrant continued surveillance?

Concerns about the threat of violence in American society are held by many people other than those responsible for the safety of American presidents and presidential candidates. As the incidence of violent crime in general has increased dramatically since 1960,[8] scholarly attention has slowly focused on the violent offender and how such persons can be identified and controlled. But progress has been slow. Until recently there has been much commentary but little actual research on the problem.[9] As with assassins there is still no valid and reliable method of identifying dangerous persons who pose a threat to the general public or to themselves.[10] What are some of the difficulties?

[c] Moore had actually worked as an FBI informant on the Patty Hearst case.

Dangerousness: The Actuarial Approach

Despite the alarming increase in assassination attempts since 1963, these remain rare events in a statistical sense. Unlike the record high levels of street violence, eight serious assassination attempts since 1963 are not very many in a population of over 230 million people. Obviously, this reveals something about the effectiveness of the job the Secret Service and other security agencies are doing. But this low base rate of incidents precludes empirically based probability studies of the kind necessary to identify those persons most likely to attempt an assassination.

Actuarial models have achieved some success in identifying, in a statistical sense, the type of person most likely to become involved in ordinary violent crime: assault, murder, and armed robbery. The problem is that actuarial models of street violence do not seem to be applicable to political assassinations.[11] Consider the left column of Chart 3, the best demographic predictors of individual violence. In a statistical sense, who is the most dangerous person in America? Does such a person also represent the most serious threat to the president?

Consistent with Bernard Goetz's enraged assessment on a New York subway,[d] actuarial statistics indicate that the most dangerous person in America is a young black male with a previous record of violent offenses. Those demographic characteristics describe the person most likely to rape, murder, and rob, but such a person has yet to attack a president or a presidential candidate. And if the data were available (they are not), my guess is that few such persons would be found on the Secret Service's watch list of its most dangerous suspects. Why? No one knows. Given the long history of black oppression and of presidential indifference to it, it remains one of the mysteries of American political behavior.[12]

[d] A jury acquitted Bernard Goetz in 1987 for reasons of self-defense after he shot and wounded four black youths who accosted him. He was later convicted on an illegal-weapons charge.

CHART 3

A Ranking of Actuarial Predictors of Violent Crime and Their
Applicability to Assassins and Would-Be Assassins

Best Predictors	Applicability (n = 17)
1. Previous history of criminal violence	1 (Ray)
2. Age 18–25	5 (Torresola, Oswald, Sirhan, Bremer, and Hinckley)
3. Male	15 (all except Fromme and Moore)
4. Black	0
5. Lower social class	3 (Oswald, Ray, and Bremer)
6. Drug abuse	0
7. Low IQ	0
8. Poor education/skills	4 (Lawrence, Torresola, Oswald, and Ray)
9. Unemployment	14 (all except Booth, Weiss, and Collazo)
10. Peer influence	2 (Fromme and Moore)

Source: Adapted from FBI annual crime statistics.

To underscore the point, consider the applicability of actuarial indicators to the universe of seventeen assassins
and would-be assassins in the right-hand column of Chart
3. With the exception of being male and unemployed there
is scant demographic similarity between the ordinary violent criminal and persons who attack presidents. The best
predictor of ordinary violent crime—a previous history of
violence—applies to only one of the seventeen subjects,
James Earl Ray. Even youth has only limited applicability:
most presidential attackers were beyond the crime-prone
later teens of their street counterparts.[13]

DANGEROUSNESS: THE CLINICAL APPROACH

Most observers agree with John Monahan's often-quoted
conclusion that "a fair summary of the existing literature
on the prediction of violent behavior would be that mental

health professionals are accurate at best in one out of three predictions of violent behavior that they make."[14] Monahan's conclusion is consistent with other earlier assessments,[15] and it is empirically grounded in a handful of significant follow-up studies of mental patients who had been institutionalized as dangerous and then released by the courts.[16]

There are a number of reasons cited for this gloomy record. First, there is the dubious validity and reliability of a good number of psychological tests regularly employed as diagnostic tools. The relationship between psychometric measures and violent behavior is minimal.[17] Moreover, as the controversy surrounding the release policies at St. Elizabeths Hospital illustrates, there is no agreement about clinically relevant variables, not to mention the relationships between those variables.[18] Second, in the absence of any empirically verifiable criteria for dangerousness, there has been a well-documented tendency of psychiatrists to overdiagnose mental illness as well as the potential dangerousness of their patients.[19] When clinical interviews are successful, it is usually because of some indefinable—and, as yet, unteachable—talent possessed by the interviewer.[20] Third, there is the accompanying clinical inclination to focus on dispositional characteristics while ignoring critical situational factors that are important contributors to the subject's potential for violence.[21]

A more general problem that must also be considered is the dominant approach and paradigm of too much of behavioral science. Most research is still based on attitudinal studies of what people *say* as opposed to what they actually *do*. It is obviously much easier to study attitudes and opinions than it is to study actual behavior, and that fact undoubtedly has something to do with the dominance of this mode of research. But this easier, more convenient approach has contributed much to the barren theoretical landscape that characterizes the study of dangerousness, not to mention other vast areas of the social sciences. Un-

fortunately, even most honest people cannot accurately report what they will do in the usually stressful, unstruc-
tured situations that signal danger; they can only say what
they *intend* to do. Heroism and cowardice are difficult to
predict. Most of us like to think that we would help another
person in distress and would probably state such intentions to an interviewer. Yet one need only recall, for example, that when a jetliner hit a Washington bridge in 1982
and plunged into the icy Potomac only a handful of persons—out of the thousands of rush-hour onlookers—made
any attempt to help the survivors. If normal people are so
inherently limited in insight and ability to anticipate their
future behavior in stressful situations, can we expect any
more from those persons whose lives are, shall we say,
somewhat more disordered?

Not only are situational variables important determi-
nants of behavior, they also have a bearing on the way people answer questions and the way those answers are evaluated. Clinical examinations are usually conducted within
institutional settings where the setting itself becomes a key
factor in the subject's responses and the examiner's evaluation of those responses. If we include the possibility of cal-
culated and deliberate deception (common among persons
in institutional settings of all kinds—mental hospitals, jails,
and, even, if we can believe the sworn testimony of Oliver
North, the National Security Council), self-reported information regarding criminal behavior, especially serious violence or one's willingness to commit a violent act in the
future, is probably unreliable. Also, it is not clear that what
is known about dangerousness within institutionalized
populations necessarily applies to those dangerous persons roaming the streets. Self-reported information—or
"attitudinal measures"—are especially uncertain guides in
assessing dangerousness, whether the attitudes are expressed in clinical interviews or registered in agree/disa-
gree fashion on pencil-and-paper tests. It is a mistake to
assume that rhetoric in any form is a valid and reliable

gauge of sentiment—and, especially, action—in unstruc-
tured situations.

In summary, the clinical approach, for all these reasons,
has yet to produce a reliable empirically based method of
assessing dangerousness. In terms of clinical criteria most
American assassins and would-be assassins did not appear
to be dangerous prior to their criminal acts. For example,
both Samuel Byck and John Hinckley were seeing psychiatrists before their attacks, as was mass murderer Charles
Whitman. None was considered dangerous, not even
Whitman, who told his psychiatrist before his attack that
he "was thinking about going up on the tower with a deer
rifle and start shooting people."[22] In most cases in which
assassins and would-be assassins were brought to trial
mental health experts could not agree on either the existence or the seriousness of mental or emotional impairment.

If these difficulties in the clinical approach are so apparent in the courtroom, is there any reason to believe that the
same approach would produce more valid and reliable information in the field? How helpful is the clinical approach
to an agent in the field when he or she is required to make
that important *short-term* prediction of whether an individual is dangerous to the president? Should the suspect be
detained for further investigation, or released?[e] How well
does that approach supplement the important but intangi-
ble skills of insight and intuition upon which such decisions are presently based? Unfortunately the clinical ap-

[e] The options available to the Secret Service are defined under Title 18 of
the United States Code, Section 3056, the so-called threat statute (18 USC
871). A person may be arrested for threatening the president or vice president. A conviction can mean up to five years' imprisonment and a one
thousand dollar fine. The Service may also seek to have such a person
committed to a mental institution if that seems appropriate. Suspicious
persons may also be "detained" for questioning while the protectee is in
the area, or placed on a watch list for continued investigation and surveillance.

proach remains almost totally dependent on self-reports that assume the suspect's willingness to answer questions truthfully. And that cannot be verified.

Assassinations are the result of a complex interaction of personality and situational variables that do not lend themselves to easy measurement and assessment. The typology of assassins (described earlier in Chart 1 and Chart 2) that emerged out of my earlier research is also, as it stands, of little use in predicting dangerousness. But that typology—because it does explore the relationship between types of assassins and would-be assassins and the particular circumstances surrounding their violent acts—provides a useful starting point for a situationally defined strategy for assessing this kind of dangerousness.

Chapter Seven

PREDICTING DANGEROUSNESS:
A SITUATIONAL APPROACH

THE CRITICAL importance of situational factors in violent behavior is now recognized, if not completely understood. In 1984, for example, John Monahan, who has defined the terms of the debate in this area, urged that actuarial studies of personal violence include clinical information as well as "situational items such as characteristics of the family environment, the work environment, and the peer group environment in which the individual is to function."[1] Definition and measurement follow recognition, and therein lies the problem. Shortly after Monahan's article appeared, two studies were published that attempted to synthesize what is known about dangerousness from both the clinical and the actuarial literature and to formulate diagnostic and predictive strategies. But neither study was able to incorporate situational variables into their models.[2] And so it remains.[3]

Also in 1984 the Committee on Research and Training Issues Related to the Mission of the Secret Service proposed a model of dangerousness. Recognizing that experience and skill in dealing with mentally ill and "violent patients" in hospitals was no substitute for experience with actual would-be assassins on the street, the committee suggested a model of dangerousness that included "five general categories that may be relevant to defining dangerousness." The categories are: "(1) interest in or motivation toward harming the protected person; (2) possession of weapons and knowledge of how to use them; (3) ability to plan an attack; (4) mobility; and (5) inhibitory factors such as a supportive family or a good job."[4]

It is a commendable beginning, perhaps, in that the categories suggest, at last, a broadened view of dangerousness that extends beyond dispositional characteristics and mental health. Still, what has been described as "the *socially constructed* nature of the dangerousness phenomenon"[5] remains elusive. That is the problem I want to address in this chapter. Before I do, let me emphasize once again that my research and the observations here are limited to only seventeen assassins or would-be assassins who have been involved in serious attacks on nationally prominent political figures. I have suggested that they constitute a small, and perhaps unique, subset of dangerous persons. I do not have access to Secret Service information about people who make threats, those who have been placed on watch lists, or "threshold cases," the persons who have been arrested before they got within striking range of their intended victims. This restriction—a restatement of the low base rate problem mentioned earlier—defines the limits of my approach.[a] But it is an approach that has not been tried on a problem that has, as yet, no solution.

How can potential assassins be identified? It is obvious that the psychological characteristics presented in Chart 1 do not set them apart from millions of other completely harmless persons who are grappling with similar concerns, problems, and afflictions. But most assassins are drawn into identifiable behavior patterns before they strike. Those patterns are suggestive of two dominant emotional states common to many of these subjects: anger and depression.

In order to consider this point, I have listed certain behavioral indicators that reflect these two emotional states. In Chart 4 the seventeen subjects are listed chronologically from left to right. The totals for each indicator are presented in the column on the extreme right. For purposes of brevity I will emphasize the modern cases, although my observations, except for those about contemporary media influences, apply to the subjects in both eras.

[a] The major risk in this approach is a familiar one in the behavioral sciences, the so-called contextual fallacy. The attempt to generalize from a few cases to a much larger population is likely to produce too many "false positive" errors—that is, designating as dangerous persons who actually are not.

CHART 4

Situational Indicators of Dangerousness

Indicators	Early Subjects, 1835–1950									Recent Subjects, 1963–1981								TOTALS
	LAW '35	BTH '65	GUT '81	CZL '01	SNK '12	ZGA '33	WIS '35	CZO '50	TSA '50	OSW '63	SRN '68	RAY '68	BRM '72	BYK '74	FRM '75	MOR '75	HNK '81	(n = 17)
Detection																		
Suspicious behavior	X	–	X	–	–	–	–	–	–	X	–	–	X	X	X	X	X	8
Weapons possession	X	X	X	X	X	X	X	–	X	X	X	X	X	–	–	X	X	14
Threats	–	–	–	–	–	–	–	–	–	X	–	–	–	X	X	X	–	4
Engagement																		
Ideological intensity	X	X	X	X	X	–	–	X	X	X	X	–	–	X	X	–	–	11
Stalking	–	X	–	X	X	–	–	–	–	–	X	X	X	–	–	–	X	7
Interest in victim	X	X	X	–	X	–	–	–	–	X	X	–	X	X	–	–	X	9
Interest in assassins	–	–	–	X	–	–	–	–	–	X	X	–	X	X	–	–	X	6
Disengagement																		
Occupational instability	X	–	X	X	X	X	–	–	X	X	X	X	X	X	X	X	X	14
Transience	X	–	X	X	X	X	–	–	–	X	–	X	X	X	X	X	X	12
Family estrangement	X	–	X	X	X	X	–	–	–	X	–	X	X	X	X	X	X	12
Attention seeking	X	–	X	–	–	–	–	–	–	X	–	–	X	X	X	X	X	8
Suicidal tendencies	–	–	–	–	–	–	–	–	–	X	–	–	X	X	–	–	X	4
Subject score	8	4	8	7	7	4	1	1	3	11	6	5	10	10	7	7	10	
	Average score = 4.7 (n = 9)									Average score = 8.3 (n = 8)								

Note: From left to right the subjects and their targets are: Richard Lawrence (Andrew Jackson), John Wilkes Booth (Abraham Lincoln), Charles Guiteau (James A. Garfield), Leon Czolgosz (William McKinley), John Schrank (Theodore Roosevelt), Giuseppe Zangara (Franklin Roosevelt), Carl Weiss (Huey Long), Oscar Collazo (Harry Truman), and Griselio Torresola (Harry Truman).

Note: From left to right the subjects and their targets are: Lee Harvey Oswald (John Kennedy), Sirhan Sirhan (Robert Kennedy), James Earl Ray (Martin Luther King), Arthur Bremer (George Wallace), Samuel Byck (Richard Nixon), Lynette Fromme (Gerald Ford), Sara Jane Moore (Gerald Ford), and John Hinckley (Ronald Reagan).

Notice that Chart 4 is divided, left to right, separating the nine early subjects (1835–1950) from the more recent (1963–1981). This chronological distinction recognizes the advent of television in the 1950s as a new and profoundly important influence in American culture. And, as I will suggest, it has become a factor that figures prominently in the motives of most recent assassins; I suggest further that the anticipation of this kind of exposure is also a factor in the growing incidence of mass public murder during the same era. The chart is divided from top to bottom into three sets of indicators comprising twelve items that can be assessed and verified empirically. Note that none of the items is solely dependent on self-reported information or the usual clinical assessment techniques.

The detection indicators refer simply to those factors that bring a suspect to the attention of a security officer: suspicious behavior in proximity to the political figure, weapons possession, or an overt threat of some type. Suspicious behavior in proximity to the intended victim is a recent phenomenon. Six of the eight recent subjects exhibited such behavior, with only Sirhan and Ray being exceptions. Only two of the nine earlier subjects, the grossly disturbed Lawrence and Guiteau, were conspicuous in this sense. What is suspicious behavior in proximity to a political figure? A wide variety of behavior qualifies as suspicious. It may be odd actions on the part of a person in a crowd awaiting the president, or something as obvious as someone detected carrying a concealed weapon. For example, Arthur Bremer, an armed regular at Wallace rallies many days and many miles apart, was very conspicuous—usually near the front of the crowd, shouting to the candidate and waving, dressed in a bizarre red, white, and blue outfit adorned with Wallace campaign buttons. Samuel Byck's picketing in front of the White House—*after* he had threatened President Nixon's life and the Israeli Embassy—was clearly suspicious, but officials didn't put the threats and the picketing together. (Or, if they did, they apparently believed they were legally powerless to do anything about Byck.) Lynette

Fromme's reputation, her well-known attempts to publicize the alleged injustice of Charles Manson's trial, combined with the bizarre red robes she wore as she waited for President Ford to pass by, could be considered suspicious behavior. Or it might be something less obvious, such as John Hinckley's appearance at the Nashville airport with three handguns in his suitcase on the day President Carter was scheduled to speak there.

All these dangerous individuals somehow were ignored or discounted as threats. No one paid any attention to Bremer until after he shot the governor; then many who traveled with Wallace, including his personal security guards, remembered seeing Bremer numerous times before. At least a few people in Washington must have cringed when they learned that Sam Byck was serious after all, that he had shot several people and then killed himself following a failed attempt to crash-dive a jetliner into the Nixon White House. Lynette Fromme summed it up for herself when she said after her arrest that *no* one ever took her seriously. And no one made anything out of the coincidence of Hinckley's and Carter's Nashville arrivals despite Hinckley's weapons. Hinckley wasn't even questioned thoroughly when his guns were confiscated. As Hinckley's mother said when she first learned of the incident—*after* his attack on President Reagan—"Why didn't anyone tell us? . . . [the police] simply confiscated the guns—fined John $60 according to the lawyer—and *informed no one.*"[6]

Prior weapons possession means little by itself among a people as well-armed as Americans. But in combination with other information, it may be important. Only three of the seventeen subjects—Oscar Collazo, Samuel Byck, and Lynette Fromme—did not own weapons prior to their attacks.

Despite the fact that a very large proportion of suspects come to the attention of authorities as a result of threats they have made, only four of the seventeen subjects actually made threats prior to their attacks. On the surface this finding alone would seem to cast doubt upon the practice of using persons who have made threats as proxies for actual assassins in statistical probability studies. Most threateners are probably very different from actual assassins, but half of the recent subjects made threats before they struck. As Oswald, Byck, Fromme, and Moore have taught us, threats cannot be ignored. Even though two of these subjects owned weapons, and all had behaved suspiciously enough to come to the attention of authorities, their actual threats were not considered serious enough for them to warrant surveillance during presidential visits. Consider, for example, Sara Jane Moore's threat—made *seeking* arrest, to both the San Francisco police and the Secret Service—that she planned to "test" President Ford's security the next day.[7] And it wasn't until after Lee Harvey Oswald killed President Kennedy that an FBI agent in Dallas remembered that Oswald had threatened to bomb the Bureau's offices less than two weeks before.

It is after a suspect comes to the attention of authorities that the other indicators—engagement and disengagement—become important in assessing whether this person constitutes a real threat or whether he or she, like so many of the persons who make threats, is merely an emotionally disturbed person seeking attention. The engagement indicators refer to those behavioral attributes that suggest anger and aggression toward a political figure: they include ideological intensity, stalking behavior, an unusual interest in the intended victim, and an unusual interest in the lives of past assassins.

Disengagement indicators suggest something about the isolation and withdrawal from ordinary social constraints that often precede violent acts. These indicators—occupational instability, transience, family estrangement, attention-seeking behavior, and suicidal tendencies—are reflective of the interpersonal difficulties, stress, and depression that characterize, especially, the Type II and Type III subjects. Let us consider the empirical and operational basis, and verifiability, of each set of indicators.

ENGAGEMENT INDICATORS

Ideological intensity. Eleven of the seventeen subjects can be described as having had a strong ideological perspective, especially subjects in the earlier era, where seven of nine can be described this way. What may seem odd is that only four of the eight more recent subjects had strong ideological perspectives; for the other half of this group ideology was unimportant. The rational basis of those perspectives varied greatly from the political extremism of Type I's like Collazo and Sirhan, through the compensatory rationalizations of the Type II's like Byck, to the delusions of the Type IV's such as Guiteau and Schrank. But rationality *per se* doesn't matter. What does matter is that such persons, for whatever reasons, often have in their possession an unusual amount of political material: books, newspaper articles, campaign literature, and the like. This material is often carried with them; it was found in trunks of cars some had used, or in quarters they had recently occupied. Such evidence is probably a much more significant indicator of ideological intensity than assessments based on interviews.

Stalking behavior. Seven of the seventeen subjects stalked their victims before attacking; half of those involved in the recent attacks were stalkers. Bus and airline ticket stubs, motel and credit card receipts, newspaper clippings from different newspapers, and, most obviously, copies of presidential or campaign schedules probably provide the best clues to this type of behavior.

Interest in the intended victim. Victim interest can be distinguished from ideological intensity, although the two may be related since the sources are often the same—newspaper and magazine articles and campaign materials. Arthur Bremer and John Hinckley, for example, had no discernible political perspective, but both had an abiding interest in the men they shot. In this sense interest refers to an unusual and enduring curiosity about the intended victim as a personality. Possession of books and articles, for example, about a president's or a candidate's personal life are one important bit of information, as are clipped newspaper, magazine, and postcard photographs. Materials of this kind were found in the possession of nine of the seventeen total subjects and five of the eight since 1963.

Interest in prior assassinations.   As time goes on and assassination attempts continue, it has become common for those contemplating such attacks to read about their predecessors or persons who have committed comparable violent crimes. Leon Czolgosz was the only assassin in the early period who was so inclined, but since then a definite pattern has emerged among five of the last eight subjects: Oswald read about Huey Long's assassination; Sirhan read about Oswald and European assassins; Bremer read about Oswald and, especially, Sirhan, and described in his diary the profound effect the film *A Clockwork Orange* had on him; Byck read about Oswald and Sirhan, as well as other Palestinian terrorists, and followed with great interest the story of rooftop sniper Jimmy Essex; and Hinckley, as we have seen, had a consuming interest in assassins and other violent persons. Again such materials are usually found among the subject's possessions, or, in some cases such as Oswald's and Sirhan's, clues to such interests were found in the form of well-used library cards. It would be unrealistic to expect to elicit important information about ongoing interest in other assassins in an interview with a suspect.

DISENGAGEMENT INDICATORS

Occupational instability.   Unemployment or marginal employment is one thing assassins and would-be assassins share with common street criminals. Fourteen of the subjects fit this characterization. All but Weiss and Collazo were underemployed. Booth's unemployment during the year preceding his assassination of President Lincoln can be considered a qualified exception in that it was not due to any decline in demand for his widely acknowledged theatrical talents. Rather, Booth chose not to work so that he could devote all of his time to the Confederate cause. All eight of the recent subjects had employment problems. Employment status is one of the easiest things to ascertain and verify; it is an integral part of any criminal investigation.

Transience. Restlessness, moving about, changing addresses, and traveling are closely linked to both occupational difficulties and emotional instability. Seven out of the eight most recent subjects and over half of their earlier counterparts lived relatively transient lives. With the exceptions of Booth, Weiss, Collazo, Torresola, and Sirhan, the remaining twelve assassins and would-be assassins frequently moved about before they struck. Transience is a little more difficult to determine than employment, but not much. It is often associated with stalking behavior, and the same evidence applies, the salient difference being that the travels of a transient do not usually coincide with the appearances of a political figure. John Hinckley, for example, traveled constantly, even before his stalks of Presidents Carter and Reagan. In these instances airline and bus ticket stubs, credit card receipts, and motel and rent receipts are usually found somewhere among the suspect's possessions.

Family estrangement. This important indicator, which characterizes twelve of the seventeen subjects and seven of the eight most recent, is also a bit more difficult to assess, but not impossible. An attempt to locate next of kin is a standard and innocuous part of most routine investigations. If the suspect identifies no one, that in itself may be important information; if someone is identified, a phone call or two may be revealing, as it would have been when John Hinckley was arrested in Nashville. Given the circumstances of his arrest, a call and interview with his parents might have revealed significant information about what he had been doing, or *not* doing, for the past few months. To an informed and perceptive investigator that could have shed additional light on whether John Hinckley had something other than a visit to Opryland on his mind that day. The fact that Lee Harvey Oswald's and Samuel Byck's family difficulties were not linked by authorities to their threats and other aggressive activities suggests another aspect of the problem. Not only should such information be sought, it must also be carefully weighed for what it might suggest about future behavior.

Attention-seeking behavior. This attribute is particularly striking among the recent subjects and relates, often directly, to the importance of publicity—especially televised publicity—in the assassins' motives. Of the earlier nine subjects only the bizarre and insane antics of Lawrence and Guiteau qualify, but a different pattern emerges from 1963 on, where every subject except Ray and Sirhan was involved in some form of attention-seeking behavior. These included: Lee Harvey Oswald's picketing and media activities on behalf of his bogus Fair Play for Cuba organization and the threat made to the FBI; Arthur Bremer's bizarre dress and behavior at Wallace rallies; Samuel Byck's threats and picketing in front of the White House, letters to newspapers, as well as the tapes he made for distribution after his death; Lynette Fromme's many, and varied, efforts to attract media attention to Charles Manson's plight; and Sara Jane Moore's not so subtle plea to have herself arrested by making an explicit threat. While these all were well-documented and relatively public activities that reflect the concerns and sensitivities of these particular subjects, attention seeking may also occur on a more private, less conspicuous level, as it did in the cases of Oswald and Byck, with their wives (and Byck's children), and Hinckley, with his parents and actress Jodie Foster.

The behavior is significant because it is linked so closely with, especially, the motives of Type II and Type III subjects who in their rejection and frustration are eventually drawn to commit commanding acts that can no longer be ignored. This kind of highly neurotic behavior should not be confused with the motives of Type I subjects—namely Czolgosz, Collazo and Torresola, and Sirhan—who sought through their attacks to focus public attention on specific political issues. In an operational sense the public side of attention-seeking behavior is self-evident; the private side is more difficult to determine. Certain hints of these activities and frustrations may be observed when a suspect is questioned; but more likely the information will come from an estranged wife, parents, or a significant third party, such as the object of the subject's romantic interest or a mental health counselor.

Suicidal tendencies. Suicide or suicidal gestures may be a form of attention-seeking behavior. Suicidal tendencies are a characteristic of more recent subjects. Half of the modern-era subjects of this study—Oswald, Bremer, Byck, and Hinckley—displayed moderate to strong suicidal tendencies. Indeed, the assassination attempts of Bremer, Byck, and Hinckley can themselves be considered suicide attempts because each expected to die. Information of this kind is usually the most difficult to attain. The only sources are police or medical records (Oswald and Byck) or the reports of family members or friends (Hinckley). In all four cases the suicidal considerations were also recorded by the subjects in diaries; in Bremer's case his diary represents the only source of evidence.

It should be apparent that none of these indicators taken alone is very revealing of anything, let alone a suspect's dangerousness. It is the total score that is (or may be) significant. In Chart 5 the seventeen subjects—all of whom were of course dangerous—are ranked according to their total scores on these combined indicators.

The purpose of Chart 5 is merely heuristic, to suggest the possible utility of a situational approach for *short-term* predictions of dangerousness. Note, for example, that with the possible exception of Zangara the least likely assassins

CHART 5

A Rank Ordering of Dangerousness Scores: All Cases, 1835–1981

Recent Subjects (n = 8)	Early Subjects (n = 9)	Score
1. Oswald*		11
2. Hinckley*		10
3. Bremer**		10
4. Byck*		10
	5. Lawrence	8
	6. Guiteau	8
	7. Czolgosz	7
	8. Schrank	7
9. Fromme*		7
10. Moore*		7
11. Sirhan		6
12. Ray		5
	13. Booth	4
	14. Zangara	4
	15. Torresola	3
	16. Weiss	1
	17. Collazo	1

Average Score = 6.4

Note: See Chart 4 for combined indicators.

* Subjects who were known to authorities prior to their attacks.

** Bremer was noticed by authorities, but he was never questioned.

and would-be assassins (that is, those who in some sense had the most to lose) score below the average of 6.4. Again with the exception of Zangara all are either Type I or Atypical subjects. Put differently, Type I and Atypical subjects are least afflicted with either mental or emotional problems, and thus their motives are more direct and easier to understand. This obviously reflects a bias within the approach toward identifying the mentally or emotionally disturbed Type II and Type III and the psychotic Type IV suspects.

There is a justification for this bias, however. Information on political activities and affiliations is easy to get. The FBI spends a good bit of its time investigating, infiltrating, and monitoring the activities of members of political extremist groups. And the Bureau is very effective, if the present difficulties of the Communist Party USA and the Ku Klux Klan are any indication. But apart from international terrorist organizations (which pose a different kind of threat), it is precisely the disturbed Type II and Type III person who now represents the most serious security threat to political figures.

In Chart 6 notice that six of the eight recent assassins and would-be assassins fall into the two middle "disturbed" (Type II and Type III) categories. Emotionally disturbed Type II and Type III subjects *and* public mass murderers, as we have seen, seek publicity.

CHART 6

A Classification of Assassins and Would-Be Assassins since 1963

Rational——————————Disturbed——————————Irrational			
Type I	Type II	Type III	Type IV
Sirhan	Oswald	Bremer	
	Byck	Hinckley	
	Fromme		
	Moore		
		Atypical	
		Ray	

How would this situational approach work in identifying dangerous suspects? One possibility might be that a suspect whose score exceeds a certain number, perhaps the 6.4 average, would qualify for immediate preventive detention and further investigation; or, if released, such a person might be marked for future surveillance in the manner of those placed on the Secret Service's watch list. Whatever the method or cutting points used, suspects with scores as high as those of Oswald, Hinckley, Bremer, and Byck should certainly create more concern than they apparently did in the past. If someone is suicidal as well as homicidal, as Type II and Type III subjects are, the best chance of apprehending them is being able to recognize the particular life situations and behavior patterns which suggest that state of mind.

The situational approach proposed here is obviously limited by the small data base from which it is derived. And without a control group for making comparisons, its validity is clearly open to question. It would be interesting to know, for example, how the actual assassins and would-be assassins considered in this chapter compare to the ordinary suspects who come to the attention of the Secret Service, or those considered dangerous enough to be placed on their watch list, or even the eerie, but usually harmless, "White House visitors" who regularly appear at the compound gates with "messages" for the president.[8]

Despite these limitations the approach seems to offer some advantages over the present data base used for guiding these assessments—for example, the highly questionable proxy studies that use surrogates to approximate the characteristics of the actual subjects instead of the subjects themselves. It is important to emphasize that the detection, engagement, and disengagement indicators are reasonably grounded in empirically verifiable evidence, and thus the approach is much less dependent on self-reported information. Nonetheless, the situationally defined engagement and disengagement indicators are suggestive of the critical mental and emotional states that precede the violence of the most common Type II and Type III subjects (namely, frustration and anger and the probable intensity of these emotions) as well as their social isolation (which implies something about the tenuousness of customary social constraints on the suspect's behavior). Moreover, the operational simplicity of this approach would mean that assessments of dangerousness could be made more expeditiously and confidently in the field.

Note that the approach would apply only to decisions on *short-term* detention and does not address the more complex clinical/legal issues involved in diagnostic questions that must be answered in cases involving long-term institutionalization.[b] An argument can be made that if the consequences of a false-positive prediction are only short-term (that is, inappropriately detaining a suspect for only a few days instead of weeks or months), then it may well be that concern for the protectee's life should take precedence over the suspect's rights.[9]

The Secret Service spends a disproportionate amount of its time investigating people with psychological problems. Are they really dangerous? No one can be sure. Most mentally disturbed persons are not dangerous. And some persons who are dangerous have no diagnosable symptoms of mental illness. A person's dangerousness—whether or not he is mentally ill—at any given time usually depends on situational factors. And that, of course, is the problem. In 1983, for example, the Secret Service investigated approximately 4,000 suspects. Only 120 (3 percent) were labeled dangerous.[10] But if the false-negative assessments of Oswald, Byck, Fromme, Moore, and Hinckley are considered (not to mention the apparent lapse involving the failure to investigate the very suspicious behavior of Arthur Bremer over the weeks he was observed), Type II and Type III assassins seem to be the most difficult to identify.

There are obviously many variables that enter into a person's decision to kill a prominent political figure or a group of people in public. The task in the short term is to separate the important from the unimportant. The factors I have identified appear to be important, especially in identifying the danger posed by the most common, but seemingly elusive, Type II and Type III suspects. Clearly, the approach is no substitute for the sound intuitive judgments of experienced agents, but it does offer an empirical, if rudimentary, basis for decision making that could be used in conjunction with such judgments. At present such a basis does not exist.

---

[b] Some states—for example, California—have statutes providing for the commitment of mentally disturbed persons for up to seventy-two hours on the judgment of a mental health professional or a law enforcement officer that the person is dangerous to others or himself.

Chapter Eight

CONCLUSIONS

IN THE two hundred years between 1789, when George Washington became the first president of the United States, and January 1989, when the term of Ronald Reagan expired, forty men held the nation's highest office. Four of them were killed by assassins,[a] and serious attempts were made on the lives of six others.[b] Thus one of four presidents was the target of violence. Furthermore, the political careers of four presidential candidates were interrupted, or ended, by violence.[c] Add to that list of casualties the names of the Black Muslim leader Malcolm X, who was murdered in 1965, and the civil rights leader Martin Luther King, Jr., shot to death three years later, and it would be reasonable to conclude that political prominence in the United States often entails very grave risks.

Especially since 1963. In the 25 years between then and the end of President Reagan's administration in 1989 there were eight assassination attempts on the lives of nationally prominent political leaders—one more than the seven presidential elections during the same period. That's as many assassination attempts in 25 years as were recorded in all the previous 174 years of the nation's presidential history. Faced with this trend, there is growing interest in develop-

[a] They were: Abraham Lincoln in 1865, James A. Garfield in 1881, William McKinley in 1901, and John F. Kennedy in 1963.

[b] Andrew Jackson in 1835, Franklin Roosevelt in 1933, Harry Truman in 1950, Richard Nixon in 1974, Gerald Ford (twice) in 1975, and Ronald Reagan in 1981.

[c] Theodore Roosevelt in 1912, Huey Long in 1935, Robert Kennedy in 1968, and George Wallace in 1972. Although Long was not a formally declared presidential candidate at the time of his death, there can be little doubt that he was campaigning for the office.

ing more accurate methods of identifying the dangerous persons who are likely to commit these acts. It is no longer useful to interpret these angry events as acts of madness, as the jury concluded in the *United States* v. *John W. Hinckley, Jr.*

The Hinckley case draws together the two difficult issues addressed in this book—insanity and dangerousness. The testimony at that trial focused public attention on the ambiguities that characterize clinical assessments of insanity and criminal responsibility. The controversy surrounding subsequent attempts to gain Hinckley's release from a mental hospital has raised similar concerns about clinical assessments of dangerousness.

The jury's verdict of Not Guilty by Reason of Insanity stirred the first ripples of outrage that eventually swept into law the Insanity Defense Reform Act of 1984. The new law established uniform procedures for dealing with criminal defendants whose crimes are attributable to mental disease or defect; it contained an insanity standard closely modeled on the more restrictive M'Naghten rule. Among its key provisions was a shift in the burden of proof from the prosecution to the defense, placing the difficult task of erasing "reasonable doubt" squarely on the defendant. In similar spirit the act changed the release procedure, requiring that henceforth the individual—not the State—must demonstrate through a "preponderance of the evidence" that he is eligible for discharge or for conditional release.[1]

In 1983, a year before the act was signed into law by President Reagan, the United States Supreme Court held that a criminal defendant who was found not guilty by reason of insanity may be committed to a mental institution—and held there—as long as he was considered dangerous to the community.[2] The Court seemed to be suggesting that it was the *danger* posed by a mental patient rather than his sanity or insanity that was of primary concern in determining what restrictions the state might appropriately apply to control his access to the public. In so doing the Court recognized that the threat an individual poses to the public may have little to do with whether that individual is sane or insane. It seemed to be shifting the focus away from its earlier concern for patient rights and psychiatric treatment—and the conundrum of clinical testimony on the insanity question that went with it—to a concern with the public's welfare and safety. The Court seemed to be saying that a patient's right to therapy ends where public peril begins. That, in essence, is the government's present position in the Hinckley case.

As we have seen, there were a number of clues, weeks and months before he attacked the president, to John Hinckley's growing potential for violence that were either ignored or went unrecognized—despite the fact that he was under psychiatric care. But one cannot blame Hinckley's Denver psychiatrist for the "false negative" diagnosis that nearly resulted in President Reagan's assassination and left James Brady permanently disabled. The staff at St. Elizabeths Hospital has not appeared to be any more perceptive in assessing John Hinckley's mental state. Both flawed diagnoses highlight a difficult problem within the mental health profession.

John Hinckley, I have suggested, is dangerous because he has the characteristics of a Type III sociopathic assassin. He is intelligent, shrewdly manipulative, and, of course, profoundly disturbed. But he knows right from wrong and is able to control his behavior within those boundaries—when he feels like it. When he doesn't, however, there is no conscience to constrain his violent tendencies. He remains a very dangerous person because, as a sociopath, he doesn't learn from mistakes; he doesn't respond to rehabilitation. Hinckley has demonstrated that repeatedly in the past, and continues to do so.

Sociopaths like Hinckley are especially dangerous because they attempt to manipulate psychiatrists just as they do other people. What they say is often untrue, and they can lie convincingly to advance their objectives. Guilt plays no part in modifying their behavior. Sociopaths care only about themselves; they trivialize the lives of others. Compare Hinckley's superficial and self-serving remorse about James Brady to his more genuine interest in serial killer Ted Bundy.

Psychiatric assessments are still based largely on what subjects—whether they are patients or criminals—tell their doctors about themselves. As Hinckley has demonstrated, sociopaths can fake normality when seeking hospital privileges or a parole, just as they can fake insanity to avoid punishment during a trial. Prisons are filled with violent criminals who differ from Hinckley only in that they did not have the expensive legal and psychiatric talent that was summoned in his behalf.

But this assessment of John Hinckley is based on hindsight, on the awareness of his past history of violence combined with the absence of any significant change in the attitudes that contributed to that violence. The assessment—like that of his doctors—is too subjective, too open to question; it does little to help identify any verifiable characteristics of a dangerous person—especially one who is not institutionalized. It is largely for this reason that psychiatrists and psychologists are accurate in no more than one out of three predictions of violent behavior, even in institutionalized populations.[3]

Dangerousness is not a trait that can be diagnosed. It is, as I have suggested, the result of a complex interaction of personality and situational factors. It is not merely the presence or absence of any one of these factors, it is the combination that defines the volatility of the subject and his violent potential. For different reasons both actuarial and clinical approaches have thus far failed to identify this combination. And there is no consistency emerging in the results of ongoing research.[4]

A few years ago an Institute of Medicine report observed that "assassination and its prevention are an extremely complex area of human behavior that is not well understood by behavioral scientists or clinicians."[5] In this book I have proposed a new approach to this complicated problem that identifies Lee Harvey Oswald, Arthur Bremer,

Samuel Byck, Lynette Fromme, and Sara Jane Moore as dangerous individuals. Previous methods did not. It suggests that John Hinckley was a very dangerous person *before* he shot the president. His psychiatrist, his parents, and airport security officers in Nashville didn't think he was. This is not to suggest, however, that the approach offers a complete solution. It is simply an idea, another way of thinking about fairly familiar information; and there may be practical problems in implementation that I am unaware of. But it has two advantages over clinical and actuarial approaches. First, its focus on verifiable situational factors and behavior reduces the degree to which such information can be manipulated by the suspect. Second, I have shown that this lethal combination of situational/behavioral variables defines a common pattern of behavior that preceded the violence of certain previous assassins and would-be assassins. But the true value of this approach obviously depends on its as yet untested usefulness in identifying those faceless men and women who, in the future, choose to follow in the footsteps of these dangerous people.

NOTES

Prologue

1. The account of Hinckley's activities on March 30, 1981, is drawn from the "John W. Hinckley, Jr.," files of the Federal Bureau of Investigation, File No. 175–601 (1981). Hereafter cited as *FBI Files*.

2. Ibid., "Evidence from Evergreen, Colorado," pp. H29–H33, H565–H566, H1022.

3. United States v. John W. Hinckley, Jr., Cr. No. 81–3–306 (1981), testimony of Dr. Park Dietz, pp. 6520–6521. Hereafter all references to the United States v. John W. Hinckley, Jr., will be cited as *Transcripts*.

4. *Transcripts*, testimony of Dr. Park Dietz, p. 6521.

5. *FBI Files*, "Evidence from the Park Central Hotel," pp. H15–H26; also pp. 570, 664.

6. *Transcripts*, as quoted by Dr. Park Dietz, p. 6522.

7. *FBI Files*, "Evidence from the Park Central Hotel"; *Trial Record*, Government Document N–15.

8. Ibid.

9. *FBI Files*, "Evidence from the Park Central Hotel."

10. *Transcripts*, as quoted by Dr. Park Dietz, pp. 6522–6523.

11. *FBI Files*, p. 626.

12. *Transcripts*, testimony of Dr. Park Dietz, pp. 6522–6523.

13. Ibid., as quoted by Dr. Park Dietz, pp. 6524–6525.

14. *Transcripts*, Hinckley to Dr. Sally Johnson, as quoted by Dr. Park Dietz, p. 6534.

15. *Transcripts*, Hinckley as quoted by Dr. Park Dietz, p. 6528.

16. *Transcripts*, as quoted by Dr. Park Dietz, p. 6524.

17. Ibid., pp. 6524–6525.

18. *Transcripts*, Hinckley to Dr. Sally Johnson, as quoted by Dr. Park Dietz, p. 6539.

19. The account of the shooting is drawn from *FBI Files*, pp. 1–626.

20. Ibid., pp. 126–128.

21. Ibid., "Evidence Recovered from Presidential Limousine."

22. Ibid.

23. Ibid.; *Washington Post*, April 5, 1981, p. A12.

24. *FBI Files*, p. 227.

25. Ibid., pp. 519–521.

26. *Washington Post*, April 5, 1981, p. A12.

27. *FBI Files*, "Evidence from Hospitals."

28. *Washington Post*, April 5, 1981, p. A12.

29. *Time*, April 13, 1981, p. 30.

30. *Washington Post*, April 5, 1981, p. A12.

31. Ibid.

32. *FBI Files*, "Arrest and Interview Log, John W. Hinckley, Jr." (March 30, 1981), pp. 1042–1044.

33. *FBI Files*, "Evidence from the Person of John Hinckley," pp. H1–H5; "Arrest and Interview Log," p. 1043.

34. Questioning of Hinckley reconstructed on the basis of the testimony of Arthur Edward Meyers, *Transcripts*, pp. 5852–5873.

35. *FBI Files*, 175, A–311.

CHAPTER ONE
COMING OF AGE IN DALLAS

1. Jack and Jo Ann Hinckley (with Elizabeth Sherrill), *Breaking Points* (Grand Rapids, Mich.: Chosen Books, 1985), p. 11.

2. Ibid., p. 39.

3. Ibid., p. 57.

4. Ibid.

5. Ibid., p. 67.

6. Ibid., p. 40.

7. Ibid.

8. Ibid., p. 58.

9. Ibid.

10. Ibid., p. 59.

11. Ibid., p. 56.

12. Ibid., p. 59.

13. Ibid., pp. 56, 60.

14. Ibid., pp. 60–61.

15. Ibid., p. 60.

16. Ibid., p. 65.

17. Ibid., p. 59.

18. Ibid., pp. 134, 313.

19. Ibid., p. 67.

20. Ibid., p. 79.

21. Ibid., p. 66.

22. George Getschow and Brenton R. Schlender, "Friends View Parents of Hinckley as Loving, Devoted to Children," *Wall Street Journal*, April 6, 1981, p. A1.

23. *Breaking Points*, p. 68.

24. Ibid., pp. 66, 80.

25. Ibid., p. 71.

CHAPTER TWO
THE ROAD TO RUIN

1. Jack and Jo Ann Hinckley (with Elizabeth Sherrill), *Breaking Points* (Grand Rapids, Mich.: Chosen Books, 1985), p. 82.

2. Ibid., p. 84.

3. Ibid., pp. 86–87.

4. Ibid., pp. 92–93.

5. Ibid., p. 93.

6. Ibid., pp. 95–96.

7. Ibid., p. 100.

8. Ibid.

9. Ibid., pp. 49, 105.

10. United States v. John W. Hinckley, Jr., Cr. No. 81–3–306 (1981), testimony of Dr. Thomas C. Goldman, p. 4956. Hereafter all references to the United States v. John W. Hinckley, Jr., will be cited as *Transcripts*.

11. "John W. Hinckley, Jr.," files, Federal Bureau of Investigation, File No. 175–601 (1981), p. 965 and "Evidence from Evergreen, Colorado." Hereafter all references to the Hinckley files will be cited as *FBI Files*.

12. *Breaking Points*, pp. 127–128.

13. Ibid., pp. 100, 126.

14. *FBI Files*, p. 620.

15. *Transcripts*, as quoted by Dr. Park Dietz, p. 6642.

16. Ibid., pp. 6631–6635; Defense Exhibit F–7; see also *Breaking Points*, pp. 297–299.

17. *Breaking Points*, p. 128.

18. Ibid., p. 129.

19. *FBI Files*, "Evidence from Evergreen, Colorado."

20. *FBI Files*, p. 968.

21. *Transcripts*, testimony of Dr. Sally Johnson, pp. 7487–7533.

22. *FBI Files*, "Evidence from Evergreen, Colorado"; *Transcripts*, testimony of Dr. Park Dietz, pp. 6623–6624.

23. *Trial Record*, Government Exhibits 221a–221b (trip charts); see also *Transcripts*, testimony of Dr. Sally Johnson, pp. 7487–7533.

24. *Breaking Points*, pp. 130–131.

25. *Transcripts*, testimony of Dr. Park Dietz, pp. 6662–6896; see also testimony of Dr. Sally Johnson, pp. 7487–7533.

26. *Breaking Points*, pp. 131, 138–139.

27. Ibid., p. 139.

28. Ibid., p. 140.

29. Ibid.

30. Ibid., p. 142.

31. Ibid., p. 141.

32. *Transcripts*, testimony of Dr. Thomas C. Goldman, p. 5041.

33. *Breaking Points*, p. 146.

34. *Transcripts*, testimony of Dr. Thomas C. Goldman, pp. 5042–5047; see also testimony of Dr. Park Dietz, pp. 7068–7078.

35. *Breaking Points*, p. 153.

36. *FBI Files*, p. 970.

37. *Breaking Points*, p. 142.

38. *Transcripts*, testimony of Dr. John J. Hopper, p. 2556.

39. Quoted in *Breaking Points*, p. 291.

40. *Transcripts*, testimony of Dr. John J. Hopper, p. 2554.

41. *Transcripts*, testimony of Jack Hinckley, pp. 2898–2899; *Breaking Points*, pp. 160–161.

42. *FBI Files*, "Arrest and Interview Log, John W. Hinckley, Jr." (March 30, 1981).

43. See, for example, *Transcripts*, testimony of Jack Hinckley, p. 2899.

CHAPTER THREE
ON BEING MAD OR MERELY ANGRY

1. Author's interviews, Roger Adelman and Robert Chapman, April 30 and May 1, 1987.

2. United States v. John W. Hinckley, Jr., Cr. No. 81-3-306 (1981), testimony of Dr. Park Dietz, pp. 6604–6605; see also testimony of Dr. Sally Johnson, pp. 7487–7533. Hereafter all refer-

ences to the United States v. John W. Hinckley, Jr., will be cited as *Transcripts*.

3. *Transcripts*; see, for example, testimony of Dr. David Bear, pp. 3802–3811, 3936.

4. *Transcripts*, testimony of Dr. Park Dietz, pp. 6519, 6607–6608, 6957–6964.

5. Ibid., pp. 6483–6491; testimony of Dr. Sally Johnson, pp. 7487–7533; statement of Roger Adelman, p. 8465.

6. *Transcripts*, testimony of Dr. David Bear, p. 4150; statement of Roger Adelman, p. 4151.

7. *Transcripts*, testimony of Dr. Park Dietz, pp. 6607, 6639–6640.

8. Ibid., p. 6623.

9. *Transcripts*, testimony of Dr. Thomas C. Goldman, pp. 5081–5083.

10. *Transcripts*, testimony of Dr. Park Dietz, pp. 6948–6951.

11. *Transcripts*, testimony of Dr. Sally Johnson, p. 7447.

12. Ibid., pp. 7436–7452; see also pp. 7435, 8192.

13. *Transcripts*, testimony of Dr. William C. Carpenter, pp. 3445–3448, 8238–8259.

14. *Transcripts*, testimony of Dr. Sally Johnson, pp. 7453–7455.

15. *Transcripts*, testimony of Dr. David Bear, pp. 4105–4121; Government Exhibit 164.

16. *Transcripts*, remarks of Roger Adelman, p. 4122.

17. *Transcripts*, statement of Vincent Fuller, pp. 8514–8515.

18. Ibid., pp. 8514–8524.

19. *Trial Record*, Defense Exhibit U–44.

20. *Transcripts*, testimony of Dr. David Bear, pp. 4009–4025.

21. See, for example, the testimonies of Dr. Daniel Weinberger, pp. 5371–5690; Dr. Marjorie LeMay, pp. 5614–5678; and Dr. David Davis, pp. 5953–6018.

22. *Transcripts*, testimony of Dr. David Bear, p. 3956.

23. *Transcripts*, statement of Roger Adelman, pp. 3969–3971.

24. *Transcripts*; see, testimony of Dr. Daniel Weinberger, pp. 5377–5403, 5440–5455, 5478–5494; and testimony of Dr. Marjorie Lemay, pp. 5614–5652.

25. Jack and Jo Ann Hinckley (with Elizabeth Sherrill), *Breaking Points* (Grand Rapids, Mich.: Chosen Books, 1985), p. 318.

26. *Trial Record*, Government Document N–15.

27. *Transcripts*, statement of Roger Adelman, pp. 8396–8497.

28. *Breaking Points*, p. 323.

29. *Transcripts*, statement of Vincent Fuller, pp. 8502–8568.

30. Ibid., p. 8534; *Breaking Points*, pp. 134, 324.

31. *Breaking Points*, p. 330.

32. Ibid., pp. 67–68.

33. As quoted in George Getschow and Brenton R. Schlender, "Friends View Parents of Hinckley as Loving, Devoted to Children," *Wall Street Journal*, April 6, 1981, p. A1.

CHAPTER FOUR
CHANGING SIDES

1. See Glenn H. Miller, Joan A. Turkus, Thomas J. Polley, David M. Powell, Harold M. Boslow, and Joseph Henneberry, *Bolton Report* (on John W. Hinckley, Jr.) (Washington, D.C.: St. Elizabeths Hospital, July 30, 1982), pp. 15–16. Hereafter cited as *Bolton Report*.

2. *New York Times*, July 9, 1982, p. A10.

3. *Penthouse* (March 1983), p. 168.

4. "Opposition to Defendant Hinckley's *Pro Se* Motion For Conditional Relief and Other Relief," *United States District Court for the District of Columbia*, March 14, 1986, p. 5; United States v. John W. Hinckley, Jr., Cr. No. 81–306 (March 24, 1986), testimony of Dr. Joan A. Turkus, p. 15. Hereafter all references will be cited as *Court Record*.

5. Technically this is a patient-initiated motion under Section 301(k) of Title 24 of the District of Columbia Code.

6. *Court Record*, March 14, 1986, pp. 4, 10.

7. *Court Record*, affidavit of Joseph Henneberry, March 14, 1986, p. 2.

8. *Court Record*, testimony of Dr. Joan A. Turkus, March 24, 1986, pp. 28, 30.

9. Unlike Hinckley's earlier motion the same year, requesting a ward change and city privileges, his Christmas release was initiated by the hospital under Section 301(e) of Title 24 of the District of Columbia Code.

10. Associated Press Release, January 16, 1987 (emphasis added).

11. Author's interview, Roger Adelman and Robert Chapman, April 30, 1987.

12. This, like Hinckley's Christmas 1986 release, was formally initiated by the hospital.

13. *Court Record*, letter, St. Elizabeths Hospital to Criminal Division, United States District Court, March 23, 1987.

14. U. S. Attorney's Office, "Motion For An Order Compelling St. Elizabeths Hospital To Seek Court Approval Pursuant To 18 U.S.C., 4243 (f) For An Accompanied Release From The Hospital," Criminal No. 81–306, April 7, 1987.

15. *Court Record*, "Government's Supplemental Opposition To An Unaccompanied Conditional Release," April 11, 1987, pp. 9–10.

16. *Court Record*, Government Pleading, April 11, 1987, p. 11.

17. *Court Record*, testimony of Dr. Glenn Miller, April 13, 1987, pp. 20–21.

18. Ibid., pp. 25–26.

19. Ibid., pp. 27, 35–36.

20. Ibid., p. 29.

21. Ibid., p. 37.

22. Ibid., pp. 37–38.

23. Ibid., pp. 38–39 (emphasis added).

24. *Court Record*, statement of Roger Adelman, pp. 40–41.

25. *Court Record*, statement of Vincent Fuller, p. 41.

26. Ibid., p. 42.

27. *Court Record*, statement of Roger Adelman, p. 53.

28. *Court Record*, Government Exhibit 1, April 11, 1987.

29. *Court Record*, Government Pleading, April 11, 1987, p. 10.

30. *Court Record*, Miller as quoted by Vincent Fuller in "Reply to Opposition of the United States to St. Elizabeths Hospital's Application for Limited Conditional Release," April 10, 1987, p. 7.

31. *Court Record*, statement of Dr. Glenn Miller, April 13, 1987, p. 56.

32. *Court Record*, statement of Roger Adelman, April 15, 1987, p. 7.

33. Ibid., p. 10.

34. Ibid.

35. The premier was in May 1986.

36. *Court Record*, statement of Roger Adelman, April 14, 1987, pp. 13–15.

37. *Court Record*, statement of Vincent Fuller, April 15, 1987, p. 15.

38. Letter, St. Elizabeths Hospital to the United States District Court, April 15, 1987.

39. "Jodie Foster Photos Found in Hinckley's Room," *Washington Post*, April 26, 1987, p. A17.

40. "Hinckley Mail Minimized by Father," *Washington Post*, April 17, 1987, p. A1.

41. David Skidmore, *Arizona Daily Star*, April 19, 1987, p. A9; see also John Mintz, "Judge Would Weigh Freeing Hinckley," *Washington Post*, April 20, 1987, p. A1.

42. Mintz, "Judge Would Weigh Freeing Hinckley," p. A1.

43. *Final Report of the National Institutes of Mental Health Ad Hoc Forensic Advisory Panel*, September 28, 1987, esp. pp. 48–57, 70.

44. Ibid., pp. vi–vii.

45. *Court Record*, "Memorandum of Points and Authorities in Opposition to Defendant's Motion to Seal Certain Materials Submitted by the Government on August 11, 1988," August 24, 1988, esp. pp. 1–3; see also "Hinckley Letters in Legal Wrangle," *Washington Post*, August 26, 1988, p. C3.

46. *Court Record*, "John W. Hinckley, Jr.'s Opposition to the Government's Motion to Unseal Documents," August 24, 1988.

47. *Bolton Report*, p. 12 (emphasis added).

48. As quoted by Michael Lewis, "Furlough Debate Intensifies," *Washington Post*, April 15, 1987, p. A8.

CHAPTER FIVE
THE SOCIOPATHIC PERSPECTIVE:
HINCKLEY, BREMER, AND MASS MURDERERS

1. James W. Clarke, *American Assassins: The Darker Side of Politics* (Princeton, N.J.: Princeton University Press, 1982).

2. Ibid.

3. As quoted in ibid., p. 187.

4. "Penthouse Interview: John W. Hinckley, Jr.," *Penthouse* (March 1983), p. 105.

5. State of Maryland v. Arthur Herman Bremer, Cr. Nos. 12376–12379 (1972), Report of Eloise M. Agger, p. 837. Hereafter all references to the State of Maryland v. Arthur Herman Bremer will be cited as *Bremer Transcripts*.

6. *Bremer Transcripts*, Agger Report, p. 831.

7. Ibid., pp. 838–839.

8. Ibid., p. 842.

9. *Bremer Transcripts*, statement of Aziz Shihab, p. 954.

10. Arthur Bremer, *An Assassin's Diary* (New York: Harper & Row, 1972).

11. On Bremer, see Clarke, *American Assassins*, pp. 174–193.

12. Ibid., pp. 185–186.

13. Ibid., pp. 178–181.

14. Ibid., p. 182.

15. *Interview of Etta Huberty, "Acts of Violence"* (film documentary), HBO/Rainbow Broadcasting: Imre Horvath, producer (1985).

16. Clarke, *American Assassins*, p. 131.

17. Jack Levin and James Alan Fox, *Mass Murder: America's Growing Menace* (New York: Plenum Press, 1985); see also "Experts Say Mass Murders Are Rare but on Rise," *New York Times*, January 3, 1988, p. A16.

18. Levin and Fox, *Mass Murder*.

19. John Hinckley, "Regardless," as quoted by Jack and Jo Ann Hinckley (with Elizabeth Sherrill), *Breaking Points* (Grand Rapids, Mich.: Chosen Books, 1985), p. 195.

20. John Hinckley, "Pretend," as quoted in ibid., p. 195.

21. As quoted in Clarke, *American Assassins*, p. 188 (with spelling corrections and minor transposition for clarity).

22. As quoted by Dr. William Carpenter, United States v. John W. Hinckley, Jr., Cr. No. 81–3–306 (1981), p. 6569.

23. As quoted in Clarke, *American Assassins*, p. 188.

24. Ibid., pp. 187–188.

CHAPTER SIX
PREDICTING DANGEROUSNESS:
ACTUARIAL AND CLINICAL APPROACHES

1. J. W. Clarke, *American Assassins: The Darker Side of Politics* (Princeton, N.J.: Princeton University Press, 1982).

2. Institute of Medicine, *Research and Training for the Secret Service: Behavioral Science and Mental Health Perspectives* (Washington, D.C.: National Academy Press, February 1984), pp. 1–2, 10–11; and J. Takeuchi, F. Solomon, and W. W. Menninger, eds., *Behavioral Science and the Secret Service: Toward the Prevention of Assassination* (Washington, D.C.: National Academy Press, 1981), p. 25.

3. *Research and Training for the Secret Service*, p. 11; see also U.S., Congress, House, Committee on Appropriations, Subcommittee

on Treasury, Postal Service, and General Government, *Review of Secret Service Protective Measures*, 94th Cong., 1st sess., September 30 and October 1, 1975.

4. See, for example, S. H. Frazier, "On Interviewing Potentially Dangerous Persons," and K. R. Hammond, "On Assessment," in *Behavioral Science and the Secret Service*: Toward the Prevention of Assassination, ed. J. Takeuchi, F. Solomon, and W. W. Menninger (Washington, D.C.: National Academy Press, 1981), pp. 137, 175.

5. *Research and Training for the Secret Service*, p. 2.

6. See, for example, D. W. Hastings, "The Psychiatry of Presidential Assassination, Part I: Jackson and Lincoln," *The Journal-Lancet* 85 (March 1965): 93–100; "Part II: Garfield and McKinley," *The Journal-Lancet* 85 (April 1965): 157–162; and "Part III: The Roosevelts," *The Journal-Lancet* 85 (May 1965): 189–192. For an extensive review of this complete literature see *American Assassins*, chapter 1.

7. *Research and Training for the Secret Service*, p. 2.

8. In 1960 the FBI reported that a violent crime was committed every three minutes in the United States. Violent crime has risen steadily since then. In 1987 the FBI "Crime Clock" indicated that a violent crime was committed every twenty-one seconds. See *Uniform Crime Reports for the United States* (Washington, D.C.: Federal Bureau of Investigation, 1963–1987).

9. H. J. Steadman, "Predicting Dangerousness among the Mentally Ill: Art, Magic, and Science," *International Journal of Law and Psychiatry* 6 (1983): 389.

10. See, for example, D. Faust and J. Ziskin, "The Expert Witness in Psychology and Psychiatry," *Science* 1 (July 1988): 31–35; E. P. Mulvey and C. W. Lidz, "Back to Basics: A Critical Analysis of Dangerousness Research in a New Legal Environment," *Law and Human Behavior* 9, no. 2 (1985): 209–219; and S. A. Shaw, "Dangerousness and Mental Illness: Some Conceptual, Prediction, and Policy Dilemmas," in *Dangerous Behavior: A Problem in Law and Mental Health*, ed. C. J. Frederick (Rockville, Md.: National Institutes for Mental Health, 1978), pp. 153–191.

11. See, for example, J. Monahan, "Predicting Violent Behavior: A Review and Critique of Clinical Prediction Studies," in *Behavioral Science and the Secret Service*: Toward the Prevention of Assassination, ed. J. Takeuchi, F. Solomon, and W. W. Menninger (Washington, D.C.: National Academy Press, 1981), p. 131.

12. On this point see ibid.

13. Similarly, the authors of a study of 1,687 psychiatric patients concluded that the relationship between demographic variables and violent behavior was "inconsistent." See A. Rossi, M. Jacobs, M. Monteleone, R. Olsen, R. Surber, E. Winkler, and A. Wommack, "Characteristics of Psychiatric Patients Who Engage in Assaultive or Other Fear-Inducing Behaviors," *Journal of Nervous and Mental Disease* 174, no. 3 (1986): 154–160.

14. Monahan, "Predicting Violent Behavior," p. 129; for a more complete discussion of the problem see his monograph *The Clinical Prediction of Violent Behavior* (Rockville, Md.: National Institutes of Mental Health, 1981).

15. B. J. Ennis and T. R. Litwack, "Psychiatry and the Presumption of Expertise: Flipping Coins in the Courtroom," *California Law Review* 62, no. 3 (1974): 695–752; B. L. Diamond, "The Psychiatric Prediction of Dangerousness," *University of Pennsylvania Law Review* 123 (1974): 439–452; and A. Dershowitz, "The Law of Dangerousness: Some Fictions about Predictions," *Journal of Legal Education* 23 (1970): 24–46.

16. H. J. Steadman and J. Cocozza, *Careers of the Criminally Insane* (Lexington, Mass.: Lexington Books, 1974); H. J. Steadman, "A New Look at Recidivism among Patuxent Inmates," *The Bulletin of the American Academy of Psychiatry and Law* 5 (1977): 200–209; J. Cocozza and H. J. Steadman, "Prediction in Psychiatry: An Example of Misplaced Confidence in Experts," *Social Problems* 25 (1978): 265–276; and T. Thornberry and J. Jacoby, *The Criminally Insane: A Community Follow-Up of Mentally Ill Offenders* (Chicago: University of Chicago Press, 1979).

17. E. Megargee, "The Prediction of Violence with Psychological Tests," in *Current Topics in Clinical and Community Psychology*, ed. C. Spielberger (New York: Academic Press, 1970); Monahan, *The Clinical Prediction of Violent Behavior*, p. 50; and T. Holland, G. Beckett, and M. Levi, "Intelligence, Personality, and Criminal Violence: A Multivariate Analysis," *Journal of Consulting and Clinical Psychology* 49 (February 1981): 106–111.

18. Mulvey and Lidz, "Back to Basics," p. 216.

19. A classic experiment in such institutional effects on the examiners is D. L. Rosenhan, "On Being Sane in Insane Places," *Science* 179 (1973): 250–258. See also J. Rappeport and G. Lassen, "Dangerousness: Arrest Rate Comparisons of Discharged Patients and the General Population," *American Journal of Psychiatry*

212 (1965): 776–783; Baxstrom v. Herold, 383 U.S. 107 (1966), and a discussion of the results in Steadman and Cocozza, *Careers of the Criminally Insane*; Cocozza and Steadman, "Prediction in Psychiatry," pp. 265–276; and Monahan, *The Clinical Prediction of Violent Behavior*, pp. 77–82.

20. See, for example, C. Montandon and T. Harding, "The Reliability of Dangerousness Assessments: A Decision-Making Exercise," *British Journal of Psychiatry* 144 (1984): 149–155; Monahan, *The Clinical Prediction of Violent Behavior*, pp. 21–38; and J. Cocozza and H. Steadman, "The Failure of Psychiartric Predictions of Dangerousness: Clear and Convincing Evidence," *Rutgers Law Review* 29 (1976): 1074–1101.

21. For comments on the problem see H. J. Steadman, "A Situational Approach to Violence," *International Journal of Law and Psychiatry* 5 (1982): 171–186; Monahan, *The Clinical Prediction of Violent Behavior*; and M. Cohen, A. Groth, and R. Siegel, "The Clinical Prediction of Dangerousness," *Crime and Delinquency* 24 (1978): 28–39. For examples of such reductionist explanations in the literature on assassins see L. Z. Freedman, "Assassination: Psychopathology and Social Pathology," *Postgraduate Medicine* 37 (June 1965): 650–658; and Hastings, "The Psychiatry of Presidential Assassination," pts. 1–4.

22. "Text of Psychiatrist's Notes on Sniper," *New York Times*, August 3, 1966, p. A20.

CHAPTER SEVEN

PREDICTING DANGEROUSNESS: A SITUATIONAL APPROACH

1. J. Monahan, "The Prediction of Violent Behavior: Toward a Second Generation of Theory and Policy," *American Journal of Psychiatry* 141, no. 1 (January 1984): 13.

2. R. J. Menzies, C. D. Webster, and D. S. Sepejak, "The Dimensions of Dangerousness," *Law and Human Behavior* 9 (1985): 49–70; see also H. V. Hall, "Predicting Dangerousness for the Courts," *American Journal of Forensic Psychiatry* 5 (1984): 77–96.

3. For a discussion of other difficulties see, J. Monahan, "Risk Assessment of Violence among the Mentally Disordered: Generating Useful Knowledge," *Journal of Law and Psychiatry* 11 (1988): 249–257.

4. Institute of Medicine, *Research and Training for the Secret Service: Behavioral Science and Mental Health Perspectives* (Washington, D.C.: National Academy Press, February 1984), p. 30.

5. Menzies et al., "The Dimensions of Dangerousness," p. 49 (emphasis added).

6. As quoted in Jack and Jo Ann Hinckley (with Elizabeth Sherrill), *Breaking Points* (Grand Rapids, Mich.: Chosen Books, 1985), p. 31 (emphasis added).

7. For a discussion of this incident and the overall problem see U.S., Congress, House, Committee on Appropriations, Subcommittee on Treasury, Postal Service, and General Government, *Review of Secret Service Protective Measures*, 94th Cong., 1st sess., September 30 and October 1, 1975.

8. For research on White House "visitors" who have been hospitalized see D. Shore, C. R. Filson, and W. E. Johnson, "Violent Crime Arrests and Paranoid Schizophrenia: The White House Case Studies," *Schizophrenia Bulletin* 14, no. 2 (1988): 279–281; D. Shore, C. R. Filson, T. S. Davis, G. Olivos, and R. J. Wyatt, "White House Cases: Psychiatric Patients and the Secret Service," *American Journal of Psychiatry* 142 (1985): 308–312; and J. A. Sebastiani and J. L. Foy, "Psychotic Visitors to the White House," *American Journal of Psychiatry* 122 (1965): 679–686. Unfortunately, for my purposes, each utilized only clinical and/or demographic information.

9. For this perspective see D. Klassen and W. A. O'Connor, "A Prospective Study of Predictors of Violence in Adult Male Mental Health Admissions," *Law and Human Behavior* 12, no. 2 (1988): 143–158.

10. *Research and Training for the Secret Service*, pp. 10–11.

CHAPTER EIGHT
CONCLUSIONS

1. The act was instituted as ch. 4 of the Comprehensive Crime Control Act of 1984, 18 U.S.C. SS20, 3006A, 4241–4247; Fed. R. Crim. P. 12.2; Fed. R. Evid. 704(b).

2. Jones v. United States, 463 U.S. 354, 368 (1983).

3. J. Monahan, *The Clinical Prediction of Violent Behavior* (Rockville, Md.: National Institutes of Mental Health, 1981), p. 60.

4. For example, a recent review concludes that "for every study that reports increases in predictive accuracy, there is another that finds clinical assessments no better than chance. Studies concluding that the relationship between demographic factors and violence among the mentally disordered is weak can be placed side by side with equal numbers of investigations finding strong corre-

lations." See J. Monahan, "Risk Assessment of Violence among the Mentally Disordered: Generating Useful Knowledge," *Journal of Law and Psychiatry* 11 (1988): 251.

5. Institute of Medicine, *Research and Training for the Secret Service: Behavioral Science and Mental Health Perspectives* (Washington, D.C.: National Academy Press, February 1984), p. 8.

ACKNOWLEDGMENTS

I WANT to mention the names of a number of individuals who helped, or whose influence was felt, on this project. For materials on the Hinckley case itself I am indebted to Roger M. Adelman and Robert "Dick" Chapman of the United States Attorneys Office in Washington. After an introduction by my good friend, Bill White, Dick and, later, Roger gave me more help and cooperation than I had reason to expect. Not only did they and their hard-working staff readily make available to me the voluminous trial record and documents, as well as the pleadings that followed Hinckley's hospitalization, they provided office space, patiently answered my questions, and returned all my phone calls. I want them to know that the "Arizona Flash" is deeply appreciative but bears sole responsibility for what is written about Mr. Hinckley.

Particularly useful, also, was Jack and Jo Ann Hinckley's honest and revealing book (with Elizabeth Sherrill), *Breaking Points*. The book was an unexpected and valuable primary source of information on their son's troubled past. Files provided, on request, by the Federal Bureau of Investigation rounded out my main sources on the Hinckley case itself. The *Washington Post* was an important secondary source of information.

Before I decided to write this book, I was able to try out some of my ideas about identifying dangerous persons in several lectures the Secret Service invited me to give at their Washington headquarters in 1984 and 1985. In particular, my discussions with agents Mike Richardson, Ron Johnston, Ed McNally, Bob Smith, Kenny Baker, and staff psychologist Ross Siegel were useful and often enlightening.

As the endnotes in later chapters suggest, my thinking about predicting violent behavior was especially informed by the work of two distinguished scholars, John Monahan,

Professor of Law and Psychology at the University of Virginia, and Henry J. Steadman of the New York State Department of Mental Hygiene. I am also grateful to Professor James C. Davies of the University of Oregon and again to Professor Monahan for their incisive comments and helpful suggestions as this manuscript began to take shape.

My own ideas on dangerousness were first published in 1989 under the title "Identifying Potential Assassins: Some Situational Correlates of Dangerousness" in the Sage Publications volume *Violence in America: The History of Crime*, edited by Professor Ted Gurr of the University of Maryland. This earlier piece provided the core for chapters six and seven of the present book.

Mary Sue Passe at the University of Arizona flawlessly transcribed hours of tapes after my trips to Washington. Others at the university who assisted in a variety of ways were: Jamal Hosseini, Denise Allyn, Kelli-Cheyenne Waldron, Sharon Dillon, Kristina Mao, Mohammad Bahramzadeh, Bill Lockwood, Anwara Begum, and Robin Rappoport. My thanks to them all.

A special word of appreciation must be given to my editor Sanford G. Thatcher of the Princeton University Press on this the occasion of our second book together, and to Catherine Thatcher, as well, for her copyediting.

And then there are relatives: my cousin and dear friend, Bob Weston of St. Louis, who remains a continuing source of inspiration to me, whatever the task; the memory of a dear old aunt, Mayme Clark Shifflet of Charlottesville, Virginia, who, when I was a boy—and despite some evidence to the contrary—always insisted that I would amount to something someday; and my children, Julie and Michael, for loving me anyway.

My wife, Jeanne, read and critiqued earlier drafts of the manuscript over a Montana summer, but it is for her love and many kindnesses to me that I dedicate this book to her.

INDEX

Aaron, Dr. Benjamin, 10
Adelman, Roger M., 48, 57, 59, 68, 70, 71, 72
AFL-CIO union delegates, Reagan's speech to, 6
American Nazi party, 41
Asinof, Eliot, 53
assassins, sociopathic: actuarial profile of, 104–5; clinical profile of, 105–9; and interest in prior assassinations as indicator of potential dangerousness, 117; predicting dangerousness of, 99–103; presumption of mental illness among, 102, 124; situational predictors for identifying, 110–24; Type I, 81, 99, 116, 120, 121; Type II, 82–83, 84, 99, 115, 116, 119, 121, 122, 123, 124; Type III, 81, 82–83, 84, 92–98, 99, 115, 119, 121, 122, 123, 124; Type IV, 99, 116, 121
attention-seeking behavior, as indicator of potential dangerousness, 119–20

Bailey, Penny, 70
Bear, Dr. David, 51, 55, 56–57
Belfiore, Constance, 48
Benjamin, Darrell, 42
biofeedback therapy, for Hinckley, 46
Booth, John Wilkes, 15, 81, 102, 117–18
Brady, James: Hinckley as danger to, 71; Hinckley's prayers for, 67, 128; injured by Hinckley's first bullet, 8, 10, 127
Brawner rule, 50–51

Bremer, Arthur: assassination attempt on Wallace by, 41, 42, 82, 97, 103, 113, 114, 116; attention-seeking behavior of, 119; diary of, 36n, 41, 90; identified as dangerous, 128; impact of *A Clockwork Orange* on, 91–92; interest in prior assassinations, 117; as malingerer, 53; as potential mass murderer, 45; as role model for Hinckley, 41, 42, 44, 45, 53, 85–91; sexuality of, 44, 87, 89–90; socialization of, 85–91; suicidal tendencies of, 120; *Taxi Driver* based on experiences of, 88, 89, 90; trial of, 48; as Type III sociopathic assassin, 84, 85–91
Bremer, Bill, 86, 89
Bremer, Sylvia, 86, 87, 88–89
Brooks, Kib (stepfather of Jack Hinckley), 18, 60
Brownley, Dr. William, 11
bullets, "devastator," 5, 10, 59
Bundy, Ted: Hinckley's interest in, 68, 69, 70, 71, 72, 73, 74, 77, 128; as serial murderer, 94n, 128
Butner, North Carolina: Hinckley's incarceration at Federal Correctional Institute in, 54
Byck, Samuel: attempt to kill Nixon by, 82, 83, 103; attention-seeking behavior of, 113, 119; failure to identify as dangerous, 103, 108, 114, 124; family estrangement of, 119; identified as dangerous, 129; ideological intensity of, 83, 116; interest in prior assassinations, 117; motiva-